Why Read Marx Today?

'In splendidly lucid prose, Jonathan Wolff explores the continuing appeal of Marx today. Deftly sifting the living from the dead in Marx's thought, Wolff shows how his criticisms of capitalism and liberalism have lost none of their urgency, even if his communist solutions prove unconvincing.'

Professor Richard Bellamy, University of Reading

Why Read Marx Today?

Jonathan Wolff

OXFORD

UNIVERSITY PRESS

OXFORD

UNIVERSITY PRESS

Great Clarendon Street, Oxford OX2 6DP

Oxford University Press is a department of the University of Oxford.
It furthers the University's objective of excellence in research, scholarship,
and education by publishing worldwide in

Oxford New York

Auckland Bangkok Buenos Aires Cape Town Chennai
Dar es Salaam Delhi Hong Kong Istanbul Karachi Kolkata
Kuala Lumpur Madrid Melbourne Mexico City Mumbai Nairobi
São Paulo Shanghai Singapore Taipei Tokyo Toronto

with an associated company in Berlin

Oxford is a registered trade mark of Oxford University Press
in the UK and in certain other countries

Published in the United States
by Oxford University Press Inc., New York

© Jonathan Wolff 2002

The moral rights of the author have been asserted

Database right Oxford University Press (maker)

First published 2002

British Library Cataloguing in Publication Data

Data available

Library of Congress Cataloging in Publication Data

Data available

ISBN 0-19-280335-2

1 3 5 7 9 10 8 6 4 2

Typeset in New Baskerville
by RefineCatch Limited, Bungay, Suffolk
Printed and bound by TJ International Ltd, Padstow, Cornwall

Contents

Preface

In 1986 I took up a lectureship in philosophy at University College London. The duties of the post included lecturing on Marxism, within a course initially set up by my teacher, Jerry Cohen, who had recently left UCL to take up a Chair in Oxford. I enjoyed reading and thinking about Marx, and so was happy enough to take this on. But I also thought that the course probably would not survive for long. I could understand that students would like to be taught Marxism by the leading Analytical Marxist of the day, but I thought that with Jerry's departure interest in Marxism would wither away.

Well, I was wrong. The teaching of Marxism in the Philosophy Department at UCL survived Jerry's move. It also survived the fall of the Berlin Wall and has flourished in the face of the alleged deradicalization and careerism of today's students. The course is now more popular than ever, especially with US students in London for their Junior Year Abroad. This book—written at the suggestion and invitation of Shelley Cox—is based on the lectures that I have delivered over the years.

The very first draft of the book was written not in a villa overlooking Lake Como, or in a prestigious US Institute of Advanced Research, but on the London Underground: specifically the Northern and Victoria lines, scribbled into little notebooks as the trains juddered between 'non-station stops'. I can recommend the practice: it is liberating to have a reason to want the train to be delayed. And it is a want very often satisfied. Several friends read much later versions of the text, and I am particularly grateful to Terrell Carver, Jerry Cohen, Jon Pike, and Rajeev Sehgal, all of whom made valuable written comments and saved me from embarrassing errors. Writing this book has rekindled my appetite for going back again to read more and more of Marx's writings (a never-ending task). I hope that those reading this book will understand why.

Introduction

In 1907 the Italian philosopher Benedetto Croce asked 'What is living and what is dead in the thought of Hegel?' Every decade or so, someone or other gets the idea of asking the same question about Marx. Well, now it is our turn. At the start of the twenty-first century how much, if anything, will escape the funeral pyre?

My answer is: more than one might think. In recent years we could be forgiven for assuming that Marx has nothing left to say to us. Marxist regimes have failed miserably, and with them, it seemed, all reason to take Marx seriously. The fall of the Berlin Wall had enormous symbolic resonance: it was often taken to be the fall of Marxism as such, as well as of Marxist politics and economics.

But in celebrating the end of the 'evil empire' we forgot that the thinkers who inspired Eastern European communism were not evil people. On the contrary, they saw themselves as our saviours. At huge personal cost they sought to liberate humanity from what they believed to be an inhumane economic and social system: capitalism. They were fired both by a vision of how society ought to be and an account of what was wrong with existing, bourgeois, society. The positive vision turned into a nightmare (although, as we shall see, whether communist regimes were an authentic interpretation of Marx's ideas is another question). But the failure of communism does not mean that all is well with

Western, liberal, democratic capitalism. And it is Marx, above all, who still provides us with the sharpest tools with which to criticize existing society.

We can think of Marx as the great-grandfather of today's anti-capitalist movement. Of course, much has changed. For example, Marx seems to have assumed that natural resources were inexhaustible, and thus he has a much more limited ecological perspective than one would expect today. But on the other hand Marx portrays a world in which the capitalist market comes to permeate society, putting a price on everything and crowding out non-economic forms of value. Businesses grow ever-larger, becoming more ruthless and exploitative—more vampire-like—in the process. Under capitalism progress comes at a high price. As Marx himself put the point in 1856—in a speech at the anniversary of the *People's Paper*:

In our day everything seems pregnant with its contrary. Machinery, gifted with the wonderful power of shortening and fructifying human labour, we behold starving and overworking it. The new-fangled sources of wealth, by some strange weird spell, are turned into sources of want. The victories of art seem bought by the loss of character. At the same pace that mankind masters nature, man seems to become enslaved to other men or to his own infamy. Even the pure light of science seems unable to shine except on the dark background of ignorance. All our invention and progress seems to result in endowing material forces with intellectual life, and in stultifying human life into a material force. (M. 368) (For an explanation of the referencing system adopted here, see Guide to References and Further Reading.)

These, and many other, points will be explored in more detail over the course of this book. Today's critics of capitalism will still find Marx's writings to be a rich vein of source material.

Now it is one thing to be able to identify the faults in capitalism, but is quite another to be able to say what we should do instead. (It is reported that one demonstrator at a recent anti-capitalist demonstration held up a banner reading 'Replace Capitalism with Something Nice'.) Marx the creative thinker was hugely optimistic, sometimes mistaken in his arguments and assumptions, often infuriatingly vague about the details, and in consequence has little to tell us now about how to arrange society. But his criticisms of late nineteenth-century society have enormous relevance even in the early twenty-first century. We may have no confidence in his solutions, but this does not mean that the problems he identifies are not acute. This, at least, is what I shall argue here.

Reading Marx, though, is a task to be handled with care. Although sometimes regarded as a great stylist—and perhaps he is by the standards of contemporary economists and social theorists—reading the texts can be dispiriting. His great masterpiece, *Capital* Volume 1 begins with page after dry page on the definition and nature of the commodity (although patience is eventually rewarded). His early essay 'On the Jewish Question', which is possibly one of most important and influential works of political philosophy of the last two hundred years, is virtually incomprehensible to those without some knowledge of the surrounding philosophical and political context. Perhaps *The Communist Manifesto*, jointly written with Engels, is his most widely read work. This is much more accessible, but its polemical tone does not do the depth of Marx's thought real justice.

It may be true of many great thinkers, but it is certainly true of Marx, that his texts are best read when you already know, roughly, what they are going to say. Reading them with this knowledge allows one to appreciate the detail of his ideas, and often the almost breathtaking originality and quality of his mind, even in work that was left as an unfinished first draft. But at this stage you will have to take my word for it.

Many of the texts I shall discuss here are available, usually in abridged form, in the volume *Karl Marx: Selected Writings*, edited by David McLellan. Wherever possible I shall give page references to the second edition of this collection, marked as, for example (M. 123). If, as I hope, on reading this book you become inspired, if only for the moment, to read some Marx, the McLellan collection is where to start.

Marx's life and works

Marx was born in 1818, in Trier, in the German Rhineland: a part of Germany which previously had been occupied by the French under Napoleon, but more recently had been

assigned to Prussia. Marx's father, a lawyer, was born a
Jew but converted to Christianity when the anti-Jewish laws
of 1816—laws which undid Napoleonic liberalization—
required him to give up either his profession or his religion.
Marx was a precocious schoolchild, and even some of his
schoolwork has been republished in the huge Marx/Engels
Collected Works, and in the amazing internet archive
www.marxists.org. Thus one may read the seventeen-year old
Marx on 'A Young Man's Reflections on the Choice of a
Career', either in the original Latin or translated into most
major languages. After an extended and rather florid reflection upon ambition and the importance of being suited to
one's chosen career, the essay ends:

> If we have chosen the position in life in which we can most of
> all work for mankind, no burdens can bow us down, because
> they are sacrifices for the benefit of all; then we shall experi-
> ence no petty, limited, selfish joy, but our happiness will
> belong to millions, our deeds will live on quietly but perpetu-
> ally at work, and over our ashes will be shed the hot tears of
> noble people. (www.marxists.org)

A famous early letter to his father, written aged nineteen,
when a law student in Berlin, is the earliest of his better-
known work. In it Marx provides an astonishing account of
his work of the term: his poetry ('these are characteristic of
all the poems of the first three volumes that Jenny [Jenny von
Westphalen, his wife-to-be] has received from me'); his translations from classical languages; his 300-page philosophical
treatise on law; his dialogue unifying art and science; and the
barely believable quantity of law and philosophy he has read.

Thus, he says, 'during my illness I got to know Hegel from beginning to end, together with most of his disciples'. As an aside he reports that he is starting to teach himself English and Italian. The letter ends with a postscript, the first line of which has stayed with me for the twenty or more years since I first read it: 'Forgive, dear father, the illegible handwriting and bad style; it is almost four o'clock. The candle is burnt right down and my eyes are sore' (M. 9–13). One feels that Marx had already, by this time, adopted a way of working that would not change for the rest of his life.

On completion of his studies in law Marx undertook a doctorate in Philosophy, presenting a comparison of the Greek philosophers Democritus and Epicurus. But although hoping for an academic job, the intellectual company he kept was too radical, and, as an atheist to boot, there was no hope. Turning to journalism Marx continued to pursue radical and anti-governmental lines of thought, and, by 1843 was effectively forced out of Germany, moving to Paris, where he wrote some of the most important of his early writings. During this time Marx first encountered Engels, who was travelling between business in Manchester and home in Germany. By now known as a subversive and revolutionary, Marx was expelled from Paris, at the request of the Prussian authorities. With his wife and infant daughter, Jenny, he moved to Brussels in 1845, continuing his writing and developing some of the ideas about history and economics that would come to dominate his later writings.

In late 1847 'a spectre [was] haunting Europe—the spectre of Communism'. Or at least this is how Marx and

Engels opened *The Communist Manifesto* (M. 245). (The first English translation rather spoilt the effect, beginning 'A frightful hobgoblin is stalking Europe'.) Indeed by the time the work was published, in early 1848, revolutions had begun and Marx returned to Germany to play an active role, at least through his journalism. But as events played out the revolution failed and the counter-revolution soon set in. Marx returned to Paris, and then on to London in 1849, where he settled for the rest of his life.

As is well documented, Marx's life at this time revolved around his scholarly work, his involvement in political intrigue, and the basic necessity of feeding his expanding household. Sadly, only three of his six children survived infancy. Francis Wheen's recent biography is especially good on how Marx struggled to work, buttressed by credit, loans, and hack writing. So, for example, in the 1850s Marx became the London correspondent for the *New York Daily Tribune*. Many have remarked on the irony of New Yorkers receiving their analysis of British events through Marx's eyes, although by all accounts he (or rather, in many cases, Engels in Marx's name) did an excellent job. From the mid-1850s he concentrated on the economic analysis of capitalism, and after producing several published and unpublished manuscripts, finally published his masterpiece, *Capital* Volume 1, in 1867. From then on Marx continued to combine economic theory with political agitation, although his personal economic struggle had been somewhat alleviated by a legacy received in 1864. However, as his health deteriorated, and he engaged in increasing controversy with people who were potential allies,

Marx was unable to complete further volumes of his economic work, even though much was already drafted. At his death, in 1883, he left a vast mass of manuscripts. The most important of these were eventually published as *Capital* Volume 2 (1885) and Volume 3 (1894), both edited by Engels, and as three volumes of *Theories of Surplus Value* edited by the Austrian Marxist Karl Kautsky and published between 1905 and 1910. How faithful these edited works are to Marx's own thought continues to occupy scholarly debate.

The definitive edition of Marx and Engels' work, if it is ever to be completed, is the aptly named MEGA 2 edition (Marx–Engels Gesamtausgabe) in which all works are planned to be printed in their original languages. More than 100 large volumes were initially announced. An earlier, more concise, German edition runs to a mere 41 volumes. The English Language version, still in process, has already spread to more than 50 volumes, each of around 800 pages or more. It is a life's work just to read this stuff. So it is with some amusement that one reads Marx, in a letter of 1858, concerning some economic writings, saying: 'If I had the time, leisure, and means to give the whole thing the necessary finish before I hand it over to the public I would greatly condense it, as I have always liked the method of condensation' (M. 562). Incidentally, it tells of the context in which Marx wrote that in the same letter he says 'The presentation . . . is wholly scientific, hence not in violation of any police regulations in the ordinary sense' (M. 562).

Marx's works have gone through an uncountable number of editions and translations, many of which were for a long time printed and disseminated in astonishingly cheap editions produced by Soviet and Chinese state publishing houses. Now the capitalists have got in on the act too. For the centenary of Marx's death, in 1983, a rash of publishers produced new editions of *The Communist Manifesto*, hoping to cash in on the publicity, and briefly it was a best-seller. Currently more than a dozen English language editions are still announced as in print. But all sorts of editions of the works exist. I once saw an American illustrated version of *Capital* Volume 1, produced, I think, in the 1940s, in which sixty selections were each accompanied by an expressionist woodcut, although, sadly, the challenge of producing sixty engaging images of Marxist economic theory was one the illustrator failed to meet. All of the important, and many of the minor, works are now available in free, electronic editions, from www.marxists.org. Could it be that more pages of Marx have been printed than that of any other writer of non-fiction (with the exception, perhaps, of Matthew, Mark, Luke, and John)? I'll have to leave that question to others, but I'd like to know the answer.

The plan of this book

In his speech at Marx's graveside (1883), Frederick Engels, his lifelong friend, collaborator, and, sometime patron proposed that Marx's immense achievement was to make two discoveries which transformed our understanding of the social world. First, 'just as Darwin discovered the law of organic nature, so Marx discovered the law of the development of human history.' This is the theory of historical materialism. Second, 'Marx also discovered the special law of motion governing the present-day capitalist mode of production and the bourgeois society that this mode of production has created. The discovery of surplus value suddenly threw light on the problem . . . [on] which all previous investigations . . . had been groping in the dark.' This, then, is the theory of surplus value.

Rudimentary versions of these two ideas—theories of history and of economics—begin to appear in some of Marx's early writings, composed in the 1840s when Marx was still in his twenties. They were refined and developed throughout Marx's entire working life. These, we shall see in more detail, dominate his mature thought.

But Marx's early writings contain much more. His ambition, and interest, was immense, and in these writings we see Marx discussing topics, such as religion, barely mentioned later. Although Marx seemed to lose interest in some of the topics he raised this doesn't mean that we should too, and, in fact, some of the most stimulating themes are developed in these pages. Of the works that are usually referred to as the 'Early Writings'—those written in and before 1845—only a small proportion were published in Marx's lifetime. One important group of unpublished writings, variously known as the 1844 Manuscripts, the Paris Manuscripts, and the Economic and Philosophical Manuscripts—names which tell us all we need to know about place and date of composition and broad subject matter—are a combination of Marx's reading notes and subsequent reflection, apparently written in a state of great intellectual stimulation and agitation. Though largely aimed at self-clarification, they are for us a treasure trove. Marx's Early Writings will be the subject of Chapter 1 of this book. Here we will see Marx's depiction of bourgeois society as a world of alienation. Chapter 2 takes up the ideas identified by Engels; Marx's economic analysis and his theory of history, which includes his prediction that capitalism must come to an end. These, as I said, are at the centre of Marx's mature system. Chapter 3 takes stock, attempting to answer our central question: why read Marx today? Here I will argue that while we must abandon Marx's grand theories, there is still much to be learnt.

It is worth remarking, though, that the version of Marx I shall present is much influenced by Engels' understanding and presentation of Marx's work. As well as works written solely by Marx, I shall be making use of some jointly written texts (*The German Ideology* and *The Communist Manifesto*), as well as one important text written entirely by Engels (*Socialism: Utopian and Scientific*). And indeed, as we have already seen, I have taken my account of Marx's greatest achievements from Engels's speech at Marx's graveside (itself taken from a somewhat longer article on Marx written by Engels a few years earlier). Understanding Marx through Engels's eyes is nothing new, for it began in Marx's own lifetime, and hasn't stopped yet. However, scholars have always found differences between the views of Marx and Engels, and for myself I accept that the works that Engels wrote after Marx died provide little real guide to Marx's own thought. So the interpretation of Marx is still, in a sense, open. But we must start somewhere, and it is the 'Engelized' Marx—the traditional reading—with which we shall be most concerned here.

1

Early Writings

Introduction

The dominant theme of Marx's Early Writings is that the capitalist society of his day is not properly fit for human consumption. It crushes the human spirit, denying the vast majority of people any chance to develop their real potential. No existing theorist, Marx thinks, has diagnosed the human malaise correctly, and thus no one had been in any position to outline a genuine cure, although this had not stopped them trying. Marx is confident that he can do better.

In tracing out Marx's thought here we will start by looking at the criticisms of religion made by Marx's immediate philosophical predecessors, and see how Marx transforms them into a more systematic critique of society, through the development and application of the ideas of alienation and alienated labour. Along the way, we will also come to an understanding of why labour took on the importance it did for Marx. Finally, we will see why Marx thought that granting people rights of the sort we hope to enjoy in liberal regimes is not enough to bring about a truly human society. Thus, essentially, we can see three related aspects of Marx's Early Writings: his diagnosis of the ills of contemporary society; his critique of the state of existing theory; and his own attempts to provide a solution to the problems he has identified.

Religion

One reason why the works of the young Marx are so hard for us, at least at first, is that they assume that the reader is thoroughly immersed in the German politics and philosophy of the early nineteenth century. No longer a safe assumption, I fear. We have seen a sketch of the German political situation in the account of Marx's life in the previous section. But, unfortunately, the German philosophy of the day was that of Hegel and his immediate followers. Hegel has a thoroughly deserved reputation as the most difficult of the major Western philosophers, and many scholars never emerge from the thickets of his thought. So you will be as relieved as me that this is not the place to attempt to summarize his entire system.

By way of introducing the necessary background to Marx we need consider, for the moment anyway, only one aspect of Hegel's thought, and how this was taken up in the writings of a group of philosophers, many of them friends and colleagues of Marx, known as the Young Hegelians. These thinkers took inspiration from Hegel to pursue highly radical themes, which may well have been very far from Hegel's own intentions. In particular we need to pay attention to what has become known as the 'Young Hegelian theology debate'.

We start with a question from traditional theology. Why did God create the world? In fact, this is better put as the impertinent question: why did God *bother* to create the world? The world, after all, is full of wickedness and suffering. If God is perfect, and self-sufficient, why did he go to the trouble of creating anything at all outside of himself, let alone something so imperfect as the world?

Theologians had struggled with this question. Hegel proposed a novel answer. God simply would not be God without the world. This is not the trivial logical point that a ruler needs someone or something to rule over in order even to be a ruler. Rather the point is based on a general theme in Hegel's philosophy. In many cases agents cannot come to self-understanding unless and until they encounter 'the other'. Thus God, like other agents, needs to define himself in terms of an external object, which is not God. Only by engaging with and interacting with the world can God come to gain knowledge of himself. Accordingly the story of human history is equally the story of God coming to self-awareness. The Hegelian notion of 'Geist', roughly 'the spirit of the age', is also, broadly speaking 'God's current level of self-understanding'.

Part of Hegel's story is that, as he is writing, the process is nearing its completion, for it is only this fact that allows him to understand the truth. Earlier thinkers were not in a position to think the thoughts that Hegel was having, for God's self-consciousness was insufficiently developed. This also means that while other religions, such as Judaism, were obsolete hangovers from a previous immature era, Christianity is depicted as absolute truth (when suitably understood). Consequently, Hegelianism seemed to imply a type of firm religious commitment.

The Young Hegelians could not accept these claims for Christianity. The first major move was *The Life of Jesus*, written by David Strauss, published in 1835, and translated into English, like some other works of the Young Hegelians, by Mary Ann Evans, better known as the novelist George Eliot. Against the Hegelian doctrine that Christianity, and hence the gospels, represented absolute truth, Strauss shockingly proposed that the New Testament should be read on the model of the Old. That is, as a set of foundation myths. Strauss's idea was that the gospels, in their similarities and differences, represented attempts to write down an oral tradition. Consequently, the gospels were not historical narratives, but folklore.

Strauss's work sparked much debate, but the knife was twisted further with the publication of Bruno Bauer's *Kritik der evangelischen Geshichte der Synoptiker* (3 vols.: 1841–2). On the basis of close textual scholarship Bauer concluded that the gospels were not even folklore. Rather, he argued, the other gospels were all derived from Mark's. So instead of evidence of an oral tradition, we have three attempts to rewrite a single written story, and then the four were later brought together. If this is true then it seems that Christianity is simply an illusion, and those who believe it, dupes.

But if an illusion, why did it catch on so well? Ludwig Feuerbach, in *The Essence of Christianity* (1841) (also translated by George Eliot), delivered the explanation and the killer blow. Reviving a well-worked theme, Feuerbach argued that the reason why human beings resemble God is not that God created us in his image, but that we created him in ours. Although an argument known to the Ancient Greeks, it was pleasingly developed by the French Enlightenment philosopher and legal theorist Montesquieu, in his satirical *Persian Letters* (1721), which is a fanciful account of conversations between Persian travellers and their French hosts. In a memorable passage one Frenchman recounts a story of travelling through Africa, and being shocked to see that African art and sculpture depicted God as female, fat, and—heaven forbid—black. The implication is that the Africans should surely have known that God is an elderly white Frenchman, in flowing robes with a white beard. (But didn't Montesquieu know that God is an Englishman?) His friend remarks that 'it has been well-said that if triangles had a God it would have three sides'. This, essentially, is Feuerbach's point.

In Feuerbach's view we human beings have taken the powers that belong to human beings, raised them in thought to an infinite level, and then invented a being outside of us who embodies all these perfections. This God, then, is all-knowing, all-powerful, and all good (as distinct from human beings who are a little bit knowing, a little bit powerful, and a little bit good). But we bow down before this figment of our imagination rather than appreciating our qualities for what they are, and attempting to enjoy them for ourselves. This, in

Feuerbach's view, by diverting our attention and creative powers, prevents us from leading a truly human life, or creating a truly human society. Thus, according to Feuerbach, going beyond previous thinkers, we should abandon religion and replace it with a radical humanism: an understanding, enjoyment and celebration of our truly human powers, which will allow us for the first time to create a genuine community on earth.

This was the point the debate had reached as Marx was writing, and is the reason why, in 1843, he was able to open his work *Towards a Critique of Hegel's Philosophy of Right. Introduction* with the words 'the critique of religion is essentially complete' (M. 70). All this, of course, was common knowledge to the readers of the young Marx, who saw no point in going into the details, merely saying 'Man has found in the imaginary reality of heaven where he looked for a superman only the reflection of his own self.' Without knowledge of Strauss, Bauer, and Feuerbach, though, we cannot make sense of that claim.

Marx, then, accepted without question Feuerbach's contention that man has invented God in his own image. This is one of those claims that seems obviously true, and a dazzling, liberating, insight to those disposed to believe it, but a crude, insulting and subversive misrepresentation to those who do not. But we can be clear that Marx's sympathies are with those who wish to 'debunk' religion. And we should note that the significance of this debate extends far beyond academic theology. For to attack religion was also to attack the contemporary political authority which took itself to be founded on religion. This is why the atheism of the Young Hegelians posed such a threat, and why, as individuals, they could not be tolerated.

However, Marx was not content with Feuerbach's position. Once the truth was revealed, and religion exposed for the sham it is, Feuerbach felt that largely his work was done. The truth would be passed from person to person, and religion could not survive this intellectual assault. It would disappear, and human beings would be able fully to enjoy their 'species-essence'—their truly human qualities—without the distraction, and indeed the barrier, of God.

Marx believed this to be a superficial analysis. Although Feuerbach had understood the phenomenon of religion, he had not addressed its causes. But without knowing why religion had come into existence, how can we know how it can be made to disappear? Marx argues, essentially, that human beings invented religion only because their life on earth was so appalling, so poverty-stricken. This is the context of his notorious remark that 'religion is the opium of the people' (M. 72). Now for certain modern readers, this may make religion sound not too bad at all. But we have to remember that in the nineteenth century opium was a painkiller. Though, no doubt, it also had its recreational uses, its prime function was as a solace.

For example, in the later work, *Capital*, Marx comments a number of times that nursing mothers coped with their early return to the production line by stupefying their hungry babies with opiates. In one particularly disturbing footnote, Marx describes the visit of a Dr Edward Smith to Lancashire to report on the health of the cotton operatives, who were unemployed owing to a cotton crisis caused by the American Civil War. Dr Smith reported to the government that 'the crisis had several advantages. The women now had the leisure to give their infants the breast, instead of poisoning them with "Godfrey's Cordial"' (an opiate) (*Capital* 518). In another footnote, a couple of pages later, Marx quotes a Public Health Report of 1864, which says that infants who received opiates 'shrank up into little old men', or 'wizened like little monkeys' (*Capital* 522).

In sum, then, to understand this metaphor we have to understand three features of opium. First, it produces some feeling of euphoria in those that take it. Second, its common use is as a solace or relief from illness, pain, hunger or other forms of distress. Third, its regular use is very destructive; at the least it prevents the user from flourishing or thriving in a normal human way. To understand the application of the metaphor we also need to understand the ills from which religion is to bring relief. This is the torment of everyday life; consequent on industrialization which promises so much but extracts from the worker such a terrible price (as we shall soon see, in detail).

Essentially, Marx tells us that while Feuerbach has noted the symptoms of a deeper malaise, he has done nothing to understand that malaise itself. The invention of religion was not simply an unfortunate mistake, but a response to the miseries of life on earth. Removing the opium leaves us only with undisguised pain. We still need to understand and remove the defects in the world, the 'secular base'. Marx himself, in his hastily scribbled 'Theses on Feuerbach', puts the point I have just explained thus:

> Feuerbach starts out from the fact of religious self-alienation, of the duplication of the world into a religious world and a secular one. His work consists in resolving the religious world into its secular basis. But that the secular basis detaches itself from itself and establishes itself as an independent realm in the clouds can only be explained by the cleavages and self-contradictions within this secular basis. The latter must, therefore, in itself be both understood in its contradiction and revolutionized in practice. (M. 172)

We will never rid ourselves of religion, and religious alienation, until we first understand, and then remove, the condition on earth that gave rise to it. Once the cause is removed, and the disease is cured, the symptom religion will wither of its own accord. This is a vital point. Religion is not to be suppressed or abolished as such. Under the right conditions it disappears on its own. The cause, the disease, Marx argues, is alienation of a different sort, primarily alienated labour. But before we can sufficiently understand this we need to uncover a little more of Marx's philosophical background.

The philosophy of historical materialism

To understand the philosophical view that Marx adopted in his Early Writings we need to take a long run up, and through territory that might at first seem quite unconnected. But indulge me. We will cover the ground very quickly.

To begin with we need to ask a very general, even vague, question. What is the basis of the relation between the human subject and the world? One famous answer to this is Descartes's: the human mind is characterized by thought, while the essence of the world of matter is 'extension'; location in space. Thus, there is a radical division between the mind and the world, for you can be assured of your own existence as a thinking thing even when in doubt of the existence of everything else. But on this view how can you know anything, beyond the contents of your own mind? If the external world might not even exist, how can I gain any further knowledge? Notoriously Descartes could make progress only by invoking a non-deceiving God. But if his proofs of God are rejected, as they commonly are, we seem trapped in a world of pure subjectivity.

At what appears to be the opposite pole is the materialism of Thomas Hobbes. Hobbes takes human beings to be simply part of the material world. On such a conception thoughts are simply 'internal motions'. Human beings are regulated by the laws of nature, like all else, and philosophical problems become, at bottom, scientific problems. Now our topic is not whether this constitutes an answer to Cartesian scepticism, but the difficulties that arise within the Hobbesian picture itself. For once we have accepted a scientific world of nothing but molecules in motion it is very unclear what room is left for ideas of rationality, morality, and, if we want it, human freedom. Consider Hobbes's explanation of morality. Men call 'good' those things they desire, and desire is an internal movement. Hence, morality appears to be reduced to motion.

A consistent materialist might be prepared to give up ideals of rationality, morality, and freedom, but this places the materialist social critic in considerable difficulty. Consider Marx's criticism of the English utopian socialist Robert Owen, also very briefly discussed (although not by name) in the extraordinarily rich 'Theses on Feuerbach'. Owen argued that human beings are simply products of their circumstances, and so a change in circumstances is all that is necessary to change human behaviour. This view is often thought to be Marx's view too, but as we shall soon see, this is not so. Now Owen, perhaps unique among nineteenth-century socialists, had the chance to put some of his ideas in practice. Though not a politician, he was the manager of the New Lanark cotton mill, and so had the perfect opportunity to change his workers' circumstances, which he did to great effect. His workers enjoyed far superior conditions of work to those elsewhere, and productivity greatly increased too. His methods involved such things as decent housing, the first infant schools, and a reduced working day (just ten and a half hours). Just as important were innovations within the factory. Here is the example of the 'silent monitor' (replicas of which are sometimes available in the gift shop of the New Lanark Mill, which is now a museum):

> This consisted of a four-sided piece of wood, about two inches long, and one broad, each side coloured—one side black, another blue, the third yellow and the fourth white, tapered at the top, and finished with wire eyes, to hang upon a hook with either side to the front. One of these was suspended in a conspicuous place near to each of the persons employed, and

the colour at the front told the conduct of the individual during the preceding day, to four degrees by comparison. Bad, denoted by black, indifferent by blue, good by yellow, and excellent by white.

Instead of punishing his employees for a black or blue performance, Owen had his supervisors monitor their work, and each day Owen made a point of walking through the mill, inspecting the silent monitors, but saying nothing to anyone. Sure enough the workers' greatly improved their performance. Owen comments:

> Never perhaps in the history of the human race has so simple a device created in so short a period so much order, virtue, goodness and happiness, out of such ignorance, error and misery. (Morton (1969), 98–9)

Owen's modern editor remarks 'It is often said that in this, and other ways, Owen treated his work-people as children. There is some truth in this, but it must be remembered that a large proportion of them *were* children.'

Nevertheless, the criticism that Owen treated his workers as some sort of lesser beings seems spot on, even if his methods did create virtue out of misery. This leads us to Marx's own criticism. Owen wanted to change his workers by changing their circumstances, for, according to materialism, people are wholly determined by their circumstances. But how, then, do we account for Owen's own behaviour? Surely as a creature of his circumstances—much the same as anyone else of his class—he should have shamelessly exploited his workers just as any other self-respecting manager would have done. So how was he, uniquely, able to break out of the shackles of determinism? Owen himself recognized the problem and supposed that there was, luckily, a small class of individual geniuses, who are not subject to the same level of determinism. Yet this cannot be so, if determinism is true. Marx's penetrating analysis is that Owen's doctrine must divide society into two classes, one of which is superior to society, and able to change the circumstances of the masses. So Owen's materialism is not only inconsistent, it is also, in a sense, elitist.

Thus Marx rejected the crude materialism of Owen and others. Yet in fundamental philosophical terms its prime difficulty is something it shares with the picture of mind and world we saw was held by Descartes. These views have in common a theory of perception: that the mind is like a camera, recording data it receives from the external world. This we might call a representative or correspondence theory of perception.

Now it might seem that there is not much wrong with this. Isn't this what the mind does? For Marx the problem is that it is essentially a passive account. It leaves out the fact that human beings are active in the world, changing nature and what they see. The vast majority of things that one sees in the world are not simply 'there', for us to observe. Rather they are objects which have been created, or, at least, transformed, by human endeavour in one way or another.

So human beings are active in the world, not merely passive receivers of the world around them. Marx congratulates the philosophical idealists, notably Kant, for being the first to recognize this truth and to develop it in a systematic, albeit mystified, way. We can see what Marx means by considering some central elements of Kant's theory of knowledge. Kant's most innovative idea is that the human mind structures the world through categories and forms of intuition which it imposes on reality. Thus, for Kant, space and time do not exist in the world outside of us, but are 'forms of sense' which we impose on reality in perception, in order to organize and conceptualize it. We see things as related in time and space only because the human mind is constructed to see them that way. So in this sense the human mind is active. It creates the main aspects of the world around it. To some important degree the world is a human construction.

The basic insight—'mystified' by Kant, according to Marx—is that human beings at least in part create the world which they perceive. Yet Marx rejected Kant's position, endorsing some important criticisms made by Hegel, and then, in turn, criticizing Hegel. Of Hegel's various criticisms of Kant, two are most relevant here. First, for Kant, the mind has a universal, ahistoric character. The basic structure of the mind is the same in all ages and in all places. By contrast Hegel argued that the human mind developed over time, and, in different cultures existing at the same time, may have reached different levels of development. But second, and more important, the mind develops by interacting with the world. This is a 'dialectical' process. As the mind apprehends and tries to make sense of the world, it develops ever-richer and more sophisticated concepts. And as it produces such higher-level concepts it changes itself. But Hegel's view is also a form of idealism in which the mind makes up the world. As the mind changes, so does the world.

Marx thinks that Hegel has got near to the truth. The mind and the world do indeed change together. But Marx also thinks that like Kant, Hegel has mystified the real situation. For Hegel everything takes place abstractly, only on the level of thought, as the history of the development of our concepts. And this is Marx's objection.

In sum, Marx has identified and criticized two dominant philosophical traditions. Materialism, from Hobbes to Feuerbach, is flawed because of its unreflective, ahistoric character, failing to understand the role human beings play in creating the world they perceive. But it is to be praised for understanding man's continuity with the natural world. Idealism, in its final, Hegelian, form, understands the importance of historical development, but restricts this to the development of thought.

This contrast allows us to posit a rather stylized opposition between ahistoric materialism and historical idealism. Put like this, it is not difficult to see what Marx is going to take from each in order to develop a philosophy of historical materialism. Like Hegel, he accepts that man changes himself and the world through activity in the world. But unlike Hegel this transformation takes place in the practical world, as practical activity, and not merely in thought.

One key aspect of such practical activity is productive activity: labour, in other words. Kantian, and especially Hegelian, idealism is a mystified expression of the real relation between human beings and the world. Human beings find self-realization in nature. They change the world not merely by changing the way they conceptualize it but by physically transforming it: with picks and shovels; with ploughs and mechanical diggers; with looms and lathes. In changing the world they change themselves, by developing new skills, but also new needs. And this, in turn, gives rise to new forms of interaction, another aspect of our practical activity.

The idea that Marx finds missing in all previous philosophical work is that human beings have individual and collective material needs, and it is need, not individual contemplation or thought that provides human beings with their primary form of interaction with the world. In order to satisfy their needs, human beings must labour together on the world, yet in doing so they evolve evermore complex forms of production and social interaction. This engenders new needs, in a never-ending process. So a philosophical view about the interaction of human beings and nature has turned into the rudiments of a historical theory of society. And with this thought, Marx seems to believe, philosophy has finally arrived at the truth it has been striving for. Its work is done.

Labour and alienation

We can now begin to understand why labour is so important in Marx's analysis, and also why if labour is alienated this is especially disturbing. For this would mean that there is something wrong with our ability to enjoy what it is that makes us most distinctively human.

First, a quick word about the idea of alienation. In common use alienation refers to a feeling, perhaps of extreme dislocation or disorientation. This subjective idea is a part of Marx's notion of alienation, but only a small part. More fundamentally alienation is an objective fact about our lives, and we can be alienated without even realizing it. The basic idea is that two things which belong together come apart. In religious alienation, the human essence becomes 'detached' from human existence. We do not exercise our most essential features; rather we worship them, in an alien form. Overcoming alienation is a matter of bringing the two elements back into some sort of proper relation. This is the foundation of Feuerbach's radical humanism.

The idea of religious alienation, and the associated notions of 'self-alienation', and even 'alienation from species-essence' (more on this later) were well-known in advanced Young Hegelian circles. However, through his reading of political economy Marx became convinced that the alienation also applied to labour. And, as we have seen, alienated labour is a primary cause of the misery on earth that leads us to create religion, so Marx believes.

Marx's study of accounts and translations of the Scottish economist Adam Smith's *The Wealth of Nations* (first published 1776) led him to recognize several 'truths of political economy' which highlight the plight of the worker under capitalism. I should emphasize that they are derived directly from Marx's understanding of Smith, even though Smith is often thought to have been one of the leading champions of capitalism. And so he was, in a way, yet we see that he also was not blind to its deficiencies.

From Marx's jottings, we can draw out the following points that Marx claimed to have found in his reading of Smith:

1. *Under capitalism, the wages of the workers are literally minimal.* This is a consequence of the fact that the capitalist is in by far the better bargaining position, and to avoid starving the worker must be prepared to accept the very low wage that will be on offer: a wage just sufficient to keep the worker and family alive.

2. *Work is punishing.* For the same reason the worker must accept appalling conditions, leading to overwork and early death.

3. *Labour is degraded and one-sided.* As the division of labour becomes more advanced, labour becomes more machine-like, and 'from a man [the worker] becomes an abstract activity and a stomach' (Colletti 285).

4. *Labour has become a commodity.* It is bought and sold on the market like any other commodity.

5. *The worker's life has become subject to alien forces.* The demand on which the worker's life depends is founded on the desires of the wealthy and the capitalists.

Marx's innovation was to combine Smith and Feuerbach to derive an account of alienated labour. That is, the plight of the worker under capitalism is an instance of the way in which a person's essence becomes detached from his or her existence; i.e. that workers live in a way that does not express

their essence. Human beings are essentially productive crea-
tures, but, Marx alleges, under capitalism they produce in an
inhuman way. Now, to recall, the 1844 Manuscripts, in which
this discussion occurs, is an unpublished first draft, and so is
bound to contain some unclarity and can be read in more
than one way. But I shall follow what is now the standard
interpretation in which, according to Marx, there are four
chief forms of alienated labour.

The first aspect of alienated labour is alienation from the
product. There is, initially, a very straightforward understanding of this. The worker produces an object, yet has no
say or control over the future use or possession of that
object. In this sense, then, the worker, individually, is separ-
ated from, or alienated from, that product. This observation, of course, is rather banal and obvious. Things become
rather more interesting when we start to think about the
way that we collectively can become alienated from the
products we create. Two key notions are mystification and
domination.

As we have already noted, Marx makes the point that virtually everything we encounter is either created or somehow
transformed by human endeavour. This includes not only
obvious human artefacts—the pen with which I write, the
chair on which I sit—but even the 'natural' landscape
around us. As Marx remarks:

> The sensuous world ... is not a given thing direct from all
> eternity, remaining ever the same, but the product of industry
> and the state of society ... the result of the activity of a whole
> succession of generations, each standing on the shoulders of

the preceding one ... (the result of) social development, industry and commercial intercourse. (M. 190)

Consider, by way of contemporary example, the Shenandoah National Park, in Virginia, USA. A good proportion of this is now officially designated 'wilderness', as if human beings barely even know what is there. Yet earlier this century much of the area was farmland. It was converted to a national park in the 1920s and 1930s by Franklin Roosevelt's Civilian Conservation Corps, as one of a number of public works designed to tackle unemployment in the aftermath of the depression.

Now the first point is that although so much of the world is largely a human creation, we rarely think of it as such, and, in this sense, we are alienated from our products. Furthermore we often tend to take them for granted. Think of the history of engineering that was needed to make it the case that clean hot and cold water comes out of your bath taps. Yet we only take any notice when the supply has the audacity to fail. The mystification is complete when we come to reflect that so few of us really have any idea how common household objects even work. Who among us can honestly say that they understand how their refrigerator works, even when it has been explained to them? We human beings have created a world that we simply do not understand; we are strangers in our own world.

But not only are we mystified by these products, we come to be dominated by them too. Soon we will learn about Marx's theory that we are alienated in production.

Production line technology is the chief culprit. But who invented this technology, and who built it? We did. Thus it is an example of a product that dominates us.

Yet the idea of domination goes much deeper still. Consider the well-worn idea 'you can't buck the market'. We have become used to the idea that there are such things as 'market forces' and if you ignore them you do so at your peril. You are just as likely to come to grief as if you ignored natural forces—gravity, magnetism, and so on. For example, if you are a capitalist and your competitors around you start cutting prices, then you had better follow suit or you will go out of business. If your customers decide that they no longer like what you produce, then you had better produce something else, smartish.

The lesson is that the capitalist economy renders some forms of behaviour rational and others irrational. So you had better do what the market mandates or you will be in trouble. Consequently we find ourselves dominated by the market. But what is the market? Simply the accumulated effects of innumerable human decisions about production and consumption. It is, then, our own product. From which it follows that, once more, we have come to be dominated by our own product. And even though it is our own product it is not under our control. Who, for example, wants the stock market to crash? But this happens, from time to time, as an unintended consequence of our own individual actions, each one of which may have seemed perfectly rational in its own terms. The market is like a monster we have accidentally created, but which now comes to rule our lives. As Marx puts it, we experience the 'complete domination of dead matter over men' (Colletti 319).

Alienation from our product, then, is a rich idea with many strands. The next category is alienation in productive activity. This stems, we saw, from the elaborate division of labour. Now, to be clear, the problem with the division of labour is not that it splits one job into several, more specialized, tasks. Highly specialized tasks can be immensely challenging and rewarding. And whether challenging in itself or not, a task within a division of labour may also form part of joint production or teamwork, which can offer another form of fulfilment. Rather, the problem Marx discerns is that capitalist division of labour typically leads to a de-skilling of the worker, where each individual is reduced to performing a highly repetitive, mindless task, with little understanding of their place in the total process. We become little more than machines, programmed to make the same movements over and over again.

This leads us swiftly to the next category: alienation from our species-being. Now the term 'species-being' was taken from Feuerbach, but Marx gives it a new twist. The core idea stems from the question: what is it that is essential to human beings? What is it that makes them a distinctive kind of creature?

Now Marx is not interested in biological features of human beings at this point. Rather he divides the species-essence of human beings into two aspects. First, as we have already seen, the distinctive human activity is labour, or, more precisely, social productive activity. Now, of course, other animals produce too. Beavers makes dams; bees make hives. But Marx points out that human beings are capable of free production in the sense that they can produce in accordance with their will and consciousness in elaborate and unpredicted ways. There is no limit to the range of things human beings may produce. Under capitalism very few people can enjoy this aspect of their species-essence. Rather than expressing our essence in our production, we produce in a mechanical, repetitive way. It is not an enjoyment but a torment:

> The worker who for twelve hours weaves, spins, drills, turns, builds, shovels, breaks stones, carries loads, etc.—does he consider this twelve hours spinning, drilling, turning, building, shovelling, stone breaking as a manifestation of his life, as life? On the contrary life begins for him when this activity ceases, at table, in the public house, in bed. (M. 276)

The second aspect of our species-being, according to Marx, comes out in another of those 'Theses on Feuerbach', this time the sixth thesis, which contains the words: 'the human essence is no abstraction inherent in each single individual. In its reality it is the ensemble of the social relations' (M. 172). I understand this to mean that human beings are engaged in an enormous and hugely complex division of labour, that goes beyond the sphere of production narrowly so called. Our artistic and cultural achievements, our material advancement, depend on co-operation that encompasses the globe and the whole of human history. In a familiar example, it is said that there is probably not a single person on earth who could make a simple pencil. It involves so many different technologies and knowledge of diverse materials that its production is beyond the ability of any one of us, taken alone.

Consequently, although we rarely think this for ourselves, a visitor from another planet would observe that human beings are involved in an immense scheme of co-operation; making goods that will be used the world over, building on shared knowledge that has been accumulated over the ages. In any one day, a given individual may use or consume objects the production of which may have required, in the end, millions of others. This, then, reveals the social aspect of our species-essence.

Now Marx argues that we are alienated from both aspects of our species-essence under capitalism. We already briefly noted the first: that we are alienated in productive activity. We can now see that this is also a way of being alienated from our species-essence. Under capitalism the vast majority of the workforce work in a way that does not engage their distinctively human properties. Rather than exercising their creativity, their ingenuity, their ability to respond to many varying challenges and situations, they produce in a dumb, repetitive, single-track fashion. They produce as animals do, rather than as humans should. It has been said that for many workers the part of the day in which their abilities are most engaged is the drive to and from work. Thus, as we saw, Marx says many of us feel human only when we are *not* working.

The second way in which we are alienated from our species-essence merges into the final category: alienation from other human beings. Here the essential point is simply that we do not appreciate our 'species-life' for what it is. Rather than conceiving of ourselves as members of the vast scheme of co-operation just described, we think of ourselves as people who go to work to earn money, and then go to shops to spend it. We are people with tunnel vision. As Marx somewhat obscurely puts it: we use our species-life as a means to individual life. In other words the way in which we pursue our self-interest would not even be possible if we did not have a communal species-essence. Yet we utterly disregard this communal aspect of our lives. We barely give a thought to the question of who will use the things we make, and even less to how the objects we purchase came into existence. We screen everything off except our immediate consumption decision.

These are the four ways, Marx argues, in which we are alienated in our labour under capitalism: alienation from the product; in productive activity; from our species-essence, and from other people. But it doesn't stop there.

Money and credit

Money is the central part of the explanation of how alienation from other people is possible. It acts as a screen which we rarely look behind. But this is not the only adverse effect that money has. In the 1844 Manuscripts Marx also indulges in some literary criticism, reflecting upon an extended passage from Shakespeare's *Timon of Athens* and a shorter passage from Goethe's *Faust*. Marx quotes Shakespeare telling us that gold 'will make black, white; foul, fair; wrong, right; base, noble; old, young; coward, valiant' (Colletti 376).

Marx here makes a number of distinct but related points. First, there is a claim that money subverts and changes everything it touches. Money commodifies, transforms, and degrades human relations. People should be loved, for example, because they are loveable, or, perhaps, because of their family relations with others. Yet in a capitalist society, people may be loved because they are rich and others reviled because they are poor. We should admire those who command respect through their actions, their vision, or their concern for others. But, once more, we tend to admire those who are wealthy, irrespective of how they became so. Second, money is corrosive, and everything, sooner or later, has its price. Things that were once done out of a sense that this is what people should do for each other—look after our children and our elderly parents for example—we now pay others to do. The capitalistic economy is full of people paying each other to do things that were once done without thought of payment. Money, say Marx and Shakespeare, is the 'universal whore' (M. 118).

A third claim, and the one most directly derived from the Shakespeare quotation is that 'money turns all human natural qualities into their opposite' (M. 118). Now clearly this is a huge exaggeration. But underlying it is the powerful thought that in a society like ours almost anything is possible for those with enough money, but for those without it life will be a frustrating struggle. In an example of enduring relevance Marx considers education. The greatest educational resources—we all agree in theory—should be given to those most able to benefit. Yet in a pure capitalist society those with talent but no money will have no access, whereas those with money but no talent can have whatever education they wish. Needs without money will go unsatisfied; whims backed with money will be indulged.

Indeed, Marx says as a fourth point, this alienation even infects our language. Need is natural to human beings, and the human world depends entirely on people taking steps to satisfy each others' needs. Yet, Marx says, under capitalism the language of needs is debased. It becomes humiliating to ask for something on the basis that you need it; it becomes imploring, or whining.

And if this wasn't bad enough, consider the credit system, which is the money system developed perhaps to its highest level of abstraction. Here, Marx says, the decision of whether to extend credit to an individual can even be a matter of life or death for them. (One wonders whether Marx speaks from personal experience.) And in this system of finance without physical money the individual becomes the unit of currency. Consequently to obtain credit it is often necessary to be 'economical with the truth' about one's past and future. One has to counterfeit oneself. This, in turn, breeds an industry of spies and snoopers, devoted to record keeping and investigation to see who is credit 'worthy'. And here we see human language debased in another way. 'What is your net worth?' and 'How much are you good for?' are questions about wealth and credit rating, not about moral assessment of character.

The final summit is the banking system and stock market. And we have already noted what that can do to us: it can crash around our ears.

Liberalism

Marx was not the only one of his contemporaries to criticize the contemporary system in Germany. According to Marx it was backward both politically and economically. Only in philosophy was it ahead of the game. So the need was for both great political and economic change, with political reform the more urgent. For in addition to the woes it suffered in common with other advanced nations, it had its own particular difficulties too. Germany, and Prussia in particular, had discriminatory laws that many of us even find hard to comprehend today. Much of the debate centred around the 'Jewish question', for the Jews were the subject of legal discrimination, and not able to enter certain professions without renouncing their religion, as we saw in the case of Marx's father.

As the young Marx was writing, the Prussian parliament had proposed reform to end anti-Jewish discrimination. Yet the reform had been vetoed by the King, and so discrimination continued. Prussian liberals were understandably critical, continuing to call for legal equality. Yet Marx's friend and fellow Young Hegelian, Bruno Bauer, wrote two articles arguing against Jewish emancipation. Now this needs to be understood carefully. Bauer did not favour discrimination.

However, he argued that in asking for the same rights as the Christians, the Jews were asking to join in the servility that the Christians experienced. Until both Jews and Christians gave up their religion, proper emancipation for either was impossible. It was impossible to have a private life as a member of a religion—as the 'chosen people' for example—and a public life as a citizen. This, clearly, bears comparison with Feuerbach's argument that religion is a barrier to the enjoyment of our species-essence and must be transcended.

Marx's reply to Bauer in 'On The Jewish Question' is, I have already remarked, one of the great works of political philosophy, despite its apparently rather parochial concern. For Marx used the occasion to raise some fundamental issues, and this gives us the opportunity to see the depth and richness of his thought.

Many of the details of Marx's article need not concern us here. One important argument, though, is that it is patent nonsense to think that one cannot enjoy equal political rights unless religion is transcended. Marx notes that the United States gives a perfect example where religious difference does not prevent equal political participation, yet religion flourishes to a degree where 'people in the US do not believe that a man without religion can be an honest man' (M. 51). (True in some circles even today.) But Marx's real contribution begins with the distinction between political emancipation and something new: human emancipation.

Political emancipation is a matter of enjoying the 'rights of the citizen' and the 'rights of man'. Many of the rights of the citizen are focused on the process of political participation: freedom of speech, assembly, and the right to vote and to stand for public office. Other rights of the citizen include freedom of thought and of worship. The rights of man, by contrast, are considered more universal and are stated by Marx to include equality, liberty, security, and property. Thus to be politically emancipated is, essentially, to possess the liberal rights of the citizen and of man.

What, then, is human emancipation? Infuriatingly, Marx is nothing like as explicit about this as one would like. But one thing is for sure; political emancipation is not enough. We can see this by reflecting on the point that however pure and equal in its treatment of people the law may be, discrimination can nevertheless remain deep rooted in everyday life. To take an example from today, for more than thirty years it has been illegal in the UK to pay a woman less for doing the same job as a man. Yet statistics show that women are paid less than men in virtually every sphere of employment. As Marx puts it, 'the state can liberate itself from a limitation without man himself being truly free of it' (M. 51). This seems to hold for every liberal law. No law can encompass all possibilities. Without breaking the letter of the law people will find ways of employing people of their own social class, religion or race, or indulging their other prejudices.

To drive his point home, Marx makes use of a distinction between the state and civil society. The state is the realm of the citizen. In the politically emancipated state we are all equal citizens, equal before the law, proud possessors of a rich catalogue of rights, viewing each other as fellow free and equal members of the state. Yet at the level of civil society—the level of everyday economic activity—things look very different. We each seek our own advantage, competing and exploiting as necessary; jealous of the success of others and determined to hold on to what we think of as ours. Thus we each live a double life: equal public citizens and atomistic private individuals. The sad truth, according to Marx, is that atomistic civil society is the level of our real existence, while the noble level of the state is merely a collective fantasy.

We are now in a position to understand Marx's difficult view that the state is a form of alienation. Essentially the point is this. As we have seen, we are essentially communal beings, producing for each other in an immensely complex division of labour. However, under capitalism we cannot live in a properly communal way, and, typically, we do not understand or appreciate our communal essence for what it is. Nevertheless Marx seems to believe that our communal nature must express itself in some way or other: some alienated way or other.

Once religion was able to play this role. Prior to the Protestant Reformation all members of a community would be members of the same Church, praying together, and reciting phrases about everyone being equal in the eyes of the Lord. Yet with the Reformation, and the consequent fragmentation of the Church into sects, often with deep contempt for each other, religion can no longer play the role of (fake) community. But at this point the politically emancipated state comes on to the scene. Liberalism is precisely the response to religious difference. Though of different religions, we can all be equal citizens together, and thus can express our communal essence in a new, though still alienated, fashion. But the fact is that this equality is, in many contexts, merely a form of words.

Now we are ready for Marx's killer blow. Not only does political emancipation fall short of human emancipation, it is a grave obstacle. Consider again the rights of man: liberty, equality, security, and property. Liberty is the right to do as you wish as long as you don't harm others. Equality is the right to be treated by the law in the same way as everyone else. Security is the right to be protected from others, and finally, property is the right to extend this security to the enjoyment of your legitimate possessions. To be a citizen is to enjoy these rights. They are fought for and prized. Yet each of these rights, argues Marx, encourage us to view our fellow human beings as threats to us. They are rights which prescribe limits, separating each of us from others. The rights of man and the citizen are rights to preserve our atomistic existence. Accordingly they first presuppose and then reinforce our alienation from each other.

In a properly human society we would find our freedom through our relations with other human beings. A proper human life is one which is lived, at least in part, for the sake of others. Yet in the politically emancipated state the most we are offered is protection from each other. While Marx is quick to concede that this, at least, is preferable to the situation then current in Germany, when certainly not everyone received sufficient protection, nevertheless a politically emancipated state is still suffused with alienation. We can hope for a great deal more.

Emancipation

But what, precisely, can we hope for? This is one of the most disappointing and frustrating aspects of Marx's Early Writings. We know that an emancipated world will be a world without alienation, and, furthermore, it will be organized on communist lines. But this tells us very little, in itself.

Now we should not underestimate Marx's originality and depth of analysis, even so. Marx does make some vital moves. He was not, of course, the first communist, and many such ideas had been ventured before. Typically communists would propose highly elaborate schemes, planned out in fantastic detail. Presenting themselves as the great benefactors of human kind, these Utopians would commend their ideas for general approval, yet as the same time would typically be utterly clueless about how they might be implemented on anything above the smallest scale. It is said that the Utopian socialist Charles Fourier advertised that he would be available in a certain café every day, should any wealthy philanthropist be interested in discussing how they might plan out and fund an experimental version of his particular fantasy of communist society. And indeed Fourier-based communities were tried out in the United States, although they did not survive for long.

We saw that another Utopian, Robert Owen, at least had

the opportunity to put his ideas into action, at the mill he managed in New Lanark. But even he became disillusioned. The workers may have had better working and living conditions, but it would have been stretching the imagination beyond breaking point to suppose they were liberated in any real sense. Owen himself admitted this, realizing that he had failed to do very much more than raise productivity. His workers remained exploited, little more than servants at his command.

Against this background, Marx argues that communism is not to be achieved by the intellectuals, visionaries, and dreamers, but by the workers themselves. Revolution, not philanthropy and experiment, was the way ahead. Of course it had to be guided by ideas, but ideas are not enough. Inscribed on Marx's gravestone in Highgate cemetery is the final, and most famous, 'Thesis on Feuerbach', which reads: 'The philosophers have only interpreted the world in various ways; the point is to change it' (M. 158).

Marx further argues that the workers would not be fit to receive emancipation unless they were part of the struggle that brought it about.

> [Revolution] on a mass scale is necessary . . . not only because the ruling class cannot be overthrown in any other way, but also because the class overthrowing it can only in a revolution succeed in ridding itself of all the muck of ages and become fitted to found society anew. (M. 195)

Marx was the first major theorist to propose that the workers must make their own revolution. The workers will be fashioned in its fire. They will come to understand their true needs and interests, yet also their real powers and their mutual reliance. If they were to remain in the sheep-like state of workers under capitalism, communism would be a disaster. Knowledge, self-knowledge, and motivation must all change. It can change, thinks Marx, through active revolutionary struggle. Only by making the revolution will people be ready to receive it. And what will the revolution achieve? We will gather together the threads of Marx's thoughts about this later in the book once we have explored some of his other ideas.

Conclusion

For the young Marx capitalism is a regime of alienation through and through; spreading from religion, to the state, labour, money, human relations, and even language. Liberal political emancipation, in the end, makes things even worse in some respects, even though it does represent progress in many ways. Eventually existing society will be replaced by a communist system which 'transcends' our alienated state, and this will be achieved by proletariat revolution. How much of this should, and can, we believe? We will return to this in Chapter 3.

2

Class, History, and Capital

Class

We have already seen a couple of contenders for Marx's greatest soundbite: 'religion is the opium of the people'; 'the philosophers have only interpreted the world, the point is to change it'. Here is another, this time from the *Communist Manifesto*: 'The history of all hitherto existing society is the history of class struggle' (M. 246). Under capitalism, so Marx argues, society is resolving itself into the struggle between two classes: bourgeois and proletarian. The bourgeoisie are the capital owning, exploiting class, whereas the proletarian class are the workers. Thus, there are those who do the work and those who live off the work of others. While the precise form of this basic relation will change from society to society, it is, according to Marx, a near universal phenomenon. It is avoided only by those societies that are so primitive that everyone must work in order to survive, and those so advanced that they have achieved communism.

Now you may fairly ask: who are these people who are able to live off the work of others? Here, of course, we don't mean the unemployed, the elderly, or dependent family members. Rather we mean those who spend the morning banking their dividend cheques and the afternoon at the gym, on the tennis court or at the club. Or to be even more specific, we mean those who have the wealth to do this. There is a division between those who have little but their own labour to sell, and those who have the wealth (often inherited) to buy the labour of others in one form or another, even though they may also work too, because this is how they wish to live their lives. How can it be that society has organized itself along class lines? In *Capital* Marx considers the question of the origin of the division of classes under capitalism.

> [The origin of the division of the classes] is supposed to be explained when it is told as an anecdote about the past. In times long gone by there were two sorts of people; one, the diligent, intelligent, and above all, frugal elite; the other lazy rascals, spending their substance, and more, in riotous living. . . . Thus it came to pass that the former sort accumulated wealth, and the latter sort had at last nothing to sell except their own skins. And from this original sin dates the poverty of the great majority that, despite all its labour, has up to now nothing to sell but itself, and the wealth of the few that increases constantly although they have long ceased to work. Such insipid childishness is every day preached to us in defence of property. . . . In actual history it is notorious that conquest, enslavement, robbery, murder, briefly force, play the great part. (M. 521)

Now at the most superficial level, dividing society into class terms might be thought to be a merely statistical exercise. It is a matter of interest to know that people in society can be classified in this particular way; this is what we might think of as a 'census' conception of class. Just as we might want to know how many Hindus, or dentists, there are in the general population, we might also want to know how many members of the bourgeoisie there are.

However, most researchers and social scientists will want to do more with a conception of class than this. Even retailers, who might survey sizes and place people in classes 'large, medium, and small' do this not out of pure curiosity, but in order to know the ideal proportions in which to manufacture their clothes. So here we are dealing with a predictive or explanatory notion of class. People are divided into classes on one basis in order to predict or explain something else. In the retail example, we classify in terms of size in the course of predicting purchasing behaviour. Market researchers and sociologists have their own, alternative, ways of dividing society to explain and predict other features, often related to consumption behaviour.

The Marxist account of class is also intended to have an explanatory and predictive function, but of a far more significant and fundamental nature. The initial classification is made, we have already seen, on the economic grounds of what people own and what they have to do to achieve a living. Yet classes are said to 'struggle' against each other. In many cases the struggle will be a personal one: the worker wishes for higher wages and a lesser working day; the capitalist for lower wages and a longer working day. Marx observes both sides have equal right, and 'between equal rights force decides' (*Capital* 344). Many chapters of *Capital* are devoted to detailing this fight. The power lies first almost entirely with the capitalist, but with the organization of trade unions and the development of factory inspections and health and safety legislation the balance slightly shifts, although every small victory is the result of immense effort.

Part of the development of the process is the awareness among members of the proletariat that they have a common interest in measures to advance their position. Similarly the bourgeoisie come to realize that, although economically they are competitors, politically they had better form alliances to protect their collective interests. So, Marx predicts, in the course of their individual struggles both sides will develop 'class consciousness'; i.e. each person will become conscious of themselves as a member of a particular class. This now takes us to a new level, for at this point the class will be capable of acting as a class, rather than as a group of individuals who simply happen to have something in common. In this sense, for Marx, classes are real agents, which distinguishes them from the market researcher's constructions. They are much more than a handy form of classification. They are the means by which world-historical change is effected. Indeed the antagonism between the classes provides a mechanism for replacing capitalism with something more humane: communism. Only in communism can we transcend class differences. Communism will be, so it is claimed by Marx, a classless society. Our first task, though, is to set out Marx's underlying theory of history: historical materialism.

History

Marx's theory of history, according to George Bernard Shaw in his *Intelligent Woman's Guide to Capitalism and Socialism*, tells us that 'a society marches on its stomach, and its stomach greatly influences its brains'. Clearly there is a little more to the theory than this, but it is, at least, a start. What next? Here is Engels's attempt at a summary from *Socialism: Utopian and Scientific*:

> I use the term . . . 'historical materialism', to designate that view of the course of history which seeks the ultimate cause and the great moving power of all historical events in the economic development of society, in the changes in the modes of production and exchange, in the consequent division of society into distinct classes, and in the struggles of these classes against one another. (*SUS* 17)

There are several fundamentally different understandings of this theory, and if someone else had written this book you might well be presented with a quite different account. Although frustrating, this divergence in interpretation shouldn't be a surprise. Marx never spelt out his theory in full. Rather it is implicit throughout many of his writings, and needs reconstructing. The interpretation I shall follow takes as its inspiration just two pages in which Marx briefly summarizes what he describes as the 'guiding thread' of his life's work; pages later described by the Austrian Democratic Socialist, and literary executor of Engels, Eduard Bernstein (1850–1932), as a 'concise and decisive' statement of Marx's views, which has 'Never been found elsewhere with equal clearness. No important thought concerning the Marxist philosophy of history is wanting there' (*Evolutionary Socialism* 3). These pages appear in a work now known as the 1859 Preface. It was written as a preface to a book on economics called *Contribution to a Critique of Political Economy*.

The essential feature of this interpretation is that it understands Marx as presenting a systematic account of the nature of historical development, which includes firm predictions about the future course of history. Others have interpreted Marx as rather less ambitious, with many interesting observations to make about society understood historically, but with less commitment to the idea that history must follow any particular path. The 1859 Preface, however, suggests a highly systematic theory. But, you may ask, if Marx says that this is the guiding thread of his thought, why doubt its reliability as a sketch of his real view?

Critics point out, however, that the *Critique of Political Economy* was soon replaced by Marx's masterpiece, *Capital* Volume 1, and went out of print. The fact that Marx didn't reprint the Preface has led some to argue that it should not be considered so central after all. (Although, in fairness, we should note that an abbreviated version appears as a footnote in *Capital*; see *Capital* 175.) It has also been pointed out that it can hardly have been central to Marx's thought because it contains no explicit mention of class struggle. And the fact that this work had to be approved by the police censor adds further to the complications: might Marx have deliberately masked aspects of his ideas?

So there is fierce controversy over whether it is legitimate to assume that these few pages should have such weight in the interpretation of Marx. Here we shall cut through such disputes by the simple expedient of not entering them, and blithely assume that Marx meant it when he said that the theory set out represented the guiding thread of his thought. Indeed most of the things Marx says in the Preface are repeated in many other works. The novelty is that only in the Preface are they all brought together.

To understand Marx's theory it is helpful to begin with a simplified picture before we enter a few complications. Marx's leading thought is that human history is essentially the story of the development of human productive power. We human beings differ from most animals in that we act upon nature to produce the things we want and need. The driving motor of human history is the development of our methods of production, which become ever more complex, ingenious, and elaborate. In this we differ from all animals. Such development however, always takes place within some economic structure or other—slavery, feudalism, capitalism, or, one day, communism. But economic structures supplant one another. Feudalism turned into capitalism, for example. What explains this?

Marx's idea is that economic structures rise and fall as they further or impede human productive power. For a time—perhaps a very long time—an economic structure will aid the development of productive power, stimulating technological advances. Yet, Marx believes, this will typically last only so long. Eventually any economic structure (except, apparently, communism) starts to impede further growth. In Marx's terminology, it 'fetters' further development of productive power. Technology just cannot grow within the existing economic structure. At this point the economic structure is said to 'contradict' the productive forces. But this contradiction cannot continue indefinitely. There will come a time when the economic structure cannot hold out any longer, for it cannot hold up progress—the development of the productive forces—for ever. The ruling class will begin to lose its grip, and, at this point, Marx says, the economic structure will be 'burst asunder' leading to a period of social revolution. Just as one form of society is replaced by another, one ruling class falls away and another becomes dominant. This is how capitalism is said to have replaced feudalism, and will be how capitalism falls to communism.

Until the very end of the last sentence many readers, no doubt, will have found little to object to in the theory as depicted. It seems plausible enough that human history is the story of the development of human productive power. And plausible enough that forms of society rise and fall as they frustrate or impede that growth. But accept these innocent sounding claims and, it seems, you have swallowed historical materialism, and in doing so have become a Marxist. Oh.

Of course, nothing is quite so simple. It might, for example, be possible to accept the broad lines of the theory but question the predictions Marx attempted to draw. But we need more detail before we can assess anything.

So far I have mentioned two distinct elements in Marx's theory of history: first, human productive power and second the economic structure. This idea of the economic structure is best understood in terms of examples: slavery, feudalism, capitalism, communism. It is characterized by the dominant 'relation of production'. So, for example, a society where production is carried out by workers who hire out their labour power to others who have the wealth to purchase it has a capitalist economic structure. On the other hand a society where production is carried out by people who are the legal property of others has an economic structure of slavery. The particular type of class division within a society, thus, is a mark of the type of economic structure it has.

We now need to add a third element, the political and legal 'superstructure'. This includes, naturally enough, the legal and political institutions of society, such as laws, law courts, and parliamentary procedures. Marx's image of society is architectural. At the most basic, providing society's foundations, are the 'productive forces'; what we have so far called human productive power. At the next level up we have the economic structure (also, confusingly, known as the base), and, above that, the legal and political superstructure.

With these ideas in hand we can state the central claims of historical materialism with a little more precision. First there is what has been called 'the development thesis'. This we have already encountered. It says that the forces of production tend to develop over time (in other words human productive power tends to grow). We become capable of increasingly advanced production, producing more and more in less time. Next there are two 'primacy theses'.

The first states that the level of development of the productive forces within a society—its available technology—will
determine the nature of its economic structure. In Marx's
famous example from his *Poverty of Philosophy,* 'the handmill
gives you society with the feudal lord, the steam-mill gives you
society with the industrial capitalist' (M. 219–20).

Why should this be? Why should the nature of technology
available to a society determine its economic structure? In
Wage-Labour and Capital, Marx illustrates his point with a
military example:

> With the invention of a new instrument of warfare, firearms,
> the whole internal organization of the army necessarily
> changed; the relationships within which individuals can con-
> stitute an army, and act as an army, were transformed and the
> relations of different armies to one another also changed. (M.
> 281)

In other words to make an efficient use of developing technology we may have to change our patterns of work, and this
change may lead to a change in authority structures. For a
more detailed military example, consider the introduction of
a mobile field gun. Suppose three people are needed to
operate it. Now in a military context there is only one sensible way of using such a gun; put one of the three in charge of
the other two. For otherwise there may be futile, or even
damaging, disputes about when and how to use it in battle.
So one must be given the final say: power over the other two.
This, in turn, needs to be supported by a whole system of
sanctions and punishments for those who dare to disobey, if

power is going to amount to anything. Now although these relations come out very clearly in the military context, the same is true, if harder to detect, in an economy as a whole. Consider the massive and rapid development of technology during the industrial revolution. This led to ever changing methods of work, and with this, shifting customs, norms, patterns of ownership, and authority structures. On a smaller scale we see something akin to this today as the development of the internet has changed patterns of work and economic power.

This leads us to Marx's second primacy thesis, which states that the nature of the economic structure of a society determines the nature of its political and legal superstructure. The idea is that the economic power of the ruling class must be protected and consolidated, and the political and legal superstructure adjusts itself to bring this about. We have already seen a version of this thesis when looking at Marx's Early Writings. The liberal state presents itself as neutral between individuals, and a fair arbitrator between conflicting claims. For Marx this is a masquerade. The reality is that the liberal state exists to consolidate the interests of the bourgeoisie. This is the realm of Marxist social theory. Although very subtle accounts exist, the crudest are the most familiar. The hand of big business is everywhere; funding political parties; influencing the system of justice; setting electoral agendas and so on. In sum, law and politics are in the service of industrial capital. The superstructure serves the economic interests of the ruling class, thus consolidating the economic structure.

Is it really like this? If it is, why are trade unions allowed? Why do universities have Arts Faculties as well as Engineering (indeed, why allow the teaching of Marxism)? Why don't the multinationals win every one of their court cases? Marxists have an answer to this too. Although law and politics serve economic interests, it is not in the interests of the economic elite for this to be too widely known. So capitalism needs capitalists to lose a few court cases, and to allow a few people to graduate with Latin degrees, to cover its tracks. It cannot afford to be too obvious.

This will be a satisfying position to hold for those who believe it. Those who do not will be in a more frustrating position: any apparent evidence of politics and law acting against the interests of the capitalist class will be taken by Marxists as further examples of the fine job capitalism does putting people off the scent. The idea that everything can be made to confirm the truth of Marxism was ridiculed by its vitriolic critic, Karl Popper (1902–1994), who wrote of his experiences as a young student in Vienna in 1919:

> A Marxist could not open a newspaper without finding on every page confirming evidence for his interpretation of history; not only in the news, but also in its presentation—which revealed the class bias of the paper—and especially of course in what the paper did not say. (Popper 35)

Yet the sensible Marxist position is to say that real-life politics is determined by many factors, including class struggle, in which from time to time the workers—and even the intellectuals—will win out. But in the long-term the bourgeoisie will win the great majority of the important political and legal battles, at least for as long as they are economically dominant.

But let us press on. We have the development thesis (human productive power tends to grow) and the two primacy theses which together tell us that the nature of the economic structure is explained by the productive forces, and that the nature of the superstructure is explained by the economic structure. We should add, too, that the dominant ideas in society are also determined by the needs of the economic structure. As Marx says both in the *German Ideology* and the *Communist Manifesto*:

> The ideas of the ruling class are in every epoch the ruling ideas. . . . The ruling ideas are nothing more than the ideal expression of the dominant material relationships which make the one class the ruling one, therefore, the ideas of its dominance. (M. 192, 260)

Here lies the Marxist theory of ideology. So, for example, not only does this society have the institution of private property, and the surrounding fabric of property laws, we also have a very strong moral taboo against theft. Not only do we have the institution of employment, and extensive provisions of employment law, we have also internalized the attitude that unemployment—even when involuntary—is almost a moral failing. Thus not only do we see law and politics adapting to the needs of capitalism, the very ideas people have are also generated the same way. This includes ideas of morality, religion, and metaphysics (M. 180).

However compelling, or otherwise, this may be, it may, as yet, be very unclear what any of this has to do with the idea of the coming of communism. Couldn't one believe everything that has been said so far, yet have no view at all about the likelihood of communism? In fact, we have, as yet, seen almost nothing about how one form of economic structure gives way to another.

Of course, for Marx, capitalism not only has an ending but a beginning. That is, before capitalism there was feudalism. We will look at the birth of capitalism for the insight it may give us into the question of how it might die. According to the official Marxist account, feudal economic structures gave way because they were unable to develop the productive forces. They were ultimately replaced by capitalist structures, which could.

Here is the story of feudalism's sad end, according to Engels in his powerful and wonderfully readable pamphlet *Socialism: Utopian and Scientific*, and Marx in the superb final few chapters of *Capital* Volume 1. Production under feudalism—and here the discussion concerns production in the towns, not agriculture—took place within the confines of the Guild system. To produce any item and offer it for sale one had to be a member of the appropriate guild. To be a member one would have had to pay for a licence, purchased from the local lord, and licences were kept in short supply, to keep the price up, and so maximize revenues for the lord.

In consequence feudal producers were protected from competition by the law, and further protected themselves by the means of 'trade secrets' passed on only to initiates (much like the Magic Circle). Feudal handicraft, accordingly, was carried out by craftsmen and apprentices in time-honoured fashion. It was, we saw, for Marx one of the paradigms of non-alienated production.

Protected as it was, there was no internal incentive in this system for anyone to break up this cosy rhythm by the introduction of the division of labour within the production unit. Of course there was what Marx calls the social division of labour—some made chairs, some made shoes—but each craftsman would tend to make the whole object. No doubt there was some division of labour. Perhaps the apprentices did the easy bits, or the bits that didn't show, but there was nothing like the concentration on minute tasks that we see with, for example, production line techniques under capitalism.

So described it is apparent that feudalism fettered the development of human productive power. It impeded the introduction of new, highly effective, forms of production, where producing a single commodity may be the combined task of many people, each expert in their little corner of the production process. Adam Smith had been so impressed with the miracle of the division of labour that he opens *The Wealth of Nations* with an unlikely peon to a pin factory. An unskilled workman working alone, claims Smith, could barely make a single pin in a day, and certainly not more than twenty. But Smith notes that modern manufacture has broken down the production of a pin into about eighteen separate tasks, and claims that in a factory where these tasks are divided between ten men, each a specialist in just one or two, it is possible to produce 48,000 pins a day, rather than the 200 that might, at best, have been created had each worked independently. Smith argues that wherever the division of labour is introduced, production increased dramatically. (Of course, as we have seen, Smith was not blind to the stultifying effect that this had on quality of work for the worker.)

Its inability to harness the potential of the division of labour, for it had no incentive to, led to the downfall of feudalism, says Marx. For, he writes, a new class of adventurers, wealthy from its plunder of the New World and the colonies, was able to set up production outside the physical and legal confines of the feudal towns, in the seaports or countryside.

> The discovery of gold and silver in America, the extirpation, enslavement and entombment in mines of the indigenous population of that continent, the beginnings of the conquest and plunder of India, and the conversion of Africa into a preserve for the commercial hunting of blackskins, are all things which characterize the dawn of the era of capitalist production. (*Capital* 915)

Producing cheaper goods, and selling into the same markets, this new class of manufacturers eventually gained economic ascendancy, replacing the now out-moded Guild producers. This is the core of the downfall of feudalism.

Now, in the 1859 Preface Marx distinguishes the 'social revolution' from the 'ideological forms in which men become aware of this struggle and fight it out'. No doubt this distinction could be read in various ways, but one way is to postulate that Marx is making a distinction between the economic revolution, in which one type of economic structure replaces another, and the political revolution, in which a new class grasps formal political and legal authority. Accordingly, the feudal relation of the lord who licensed the Guilds was replaced by capitalist and worker. This included not only new methods of production, but new authority structures and expectations. The apprentice would have worked in the reasonable hope that one day he would become a guildsman in his own right. But any member of the proletariat who thinks that, in the natural course of events he will become a capitalist, has another think coming.

So we have seen how the economic revolution took place, at least according to Marx and Engels. But how about the political revolution? Although from the point of view of the history books, it was massively significant, Engels presents this, at least in England, as a long drawn-out sequence of relatively minor events. It began, perhaps, with the 'Glorious Revolution' of 1688, in which James II was deposed in favour of William and Mary, and the establishment of the Bill of Rights of 1689, which provided for the ascendancy of parliament over the monarch. The final victory was won in 1846, with the repeal of the Corn Laws, which had prevented the importation of corn, and thus kept corn prices, and hence the price of bread, artificially high. Presented as a victory for the workers, the real beneficiaries were the bourgeoisie, who were able to pay lower wages without starving their workers. The losers were the aristocratic landowners, who lost their protected market position and the excess profits that went with it. Slowly but surely, the rule of the aristocracy, by means of the monarch, was replaced by the rule of parliament, controlled by the capitalist class, and the creation of a 'constitutional monarch' who became no more than a figurehead. Events took a swifter and rather more exciting turn in France, of course, but to similar effect.

All the elements are now in place. Feudal economic structures fettered the development of the forces of production. When the opportunity arose, a new class attempted other types of economic relation and these were able to harness more developed productive forces, and accelerate their further development. The resulting economic revolution weakened the feudal aristocracy's political hold, and the subsequent slow-burning political revolution finally ousted them from this last remaining stronghold.

Consequently a new, capitalist, epoch was born. A capitalist economic structure was eventually combined with the rule of the bourgeoisie. In other words the superstructure consolidated and stabilized the new capitalist economic structure. Largely owing to the intrinsically competitive nature of capitalism the development of the productive forces surged ahead, and capitalism unleashed previously undreamed of technological development, which continues to this day. For, as Marx remarks in the *Communist Manifesto*: 'the bourgeoisie cannot exist without constantly revolutionizing the instruments of production' (M. 248). Innovate or die is the logic of capitalism.

Now Marx confidently believed that, just as feudalism had fettered the development of the productive forces, so, eventually, would capitalism. Indeed Marx, at times, thought that he was witnessing such a thing. Capitalist competition would turn from being an engine of technological development to a major impediment. But how could this happen? The answer lies in Marx's economic analysis of capitalism.

The economics of capitalism

Capital Volume 1, the greatest revolutionary work of the nineteenth century, an insurrectionary text of the highest order, starts with a surprisingly mundane project: 'The wealth of those societies in which the capitalist mode of production prevails presents itself as "an immense accumulation of commodities"; its unit being a single commodity. Our investigation must therefore begin with the analysis of a commodity' (M. 458).

Each commodity can be understood as a 'use-value'—that is as an object with a particular use—and as an 'exchange value'—something that can be exchanged against other commodities in particular ratios. Marx believes that the notion of use-value is relatively unmysterious, for common sense or science can tell us why commodities have the uses they do. Indeed all societies muct produce use-values (things with use-value) if they are to survive. Exchange value should strike us as a more surprising phenomenon; what explains the ratios in which commodities exchange against each other? Why should one quarter of corn have the same value as x hundredweight of iron? Marx's answer is that everything depends on how much labour was involved in making the objects (and in producing the machines used in their production, and in acquiring the raw materials from which the objects are made, and so on, and so on). In short, the quantity of the ultimate labour input explains the value of the finished commodity. Bundles of commodities with the same labour input will have the same value. This explains exchange ratios. Exchange value is a historically contingent phenomenon. For it can only occur in those societies in which exchange takes place.

To put the labour theory of (exchange) value somewhat more strictly, Marx argues that the value of a commodity is determined by the 'socially necessary' labour time required for its production. 'Socially necessary' means 'applied with the normal level of skill and exertion for that branch of industry', and is introduced to avoid the 'lazy or inefficient worker' problem. If value were determined by actual labour time then a commodity produced by a slow worker should be worth more than the identical commodity produced by a standard worker. Introducing the idea that values are proportionate not to actual labour time but to socially necessary labour time avoids this absurdity. So now we have the initial statement of Marx's labour theory of value. It is introduced as a theory of relative price (although the final picture is massively complicated by Marx's arguments in *Capital* Volume 3, which we shall leave to one side here).

Nothing very revolutionary about this so far, either in economic or political terms. The classical economists Adam Smith and David Ricardo had proposed versions of the labour theory of value before, as had many of their followers.

But Marx feels that he can offer insights that take things much further. First, although other economists had made the distinction between use-value and exchange value—what a product can be used for, and what it can be sold for— Marx claims that labour must also be considered in a double-aspect if it is to create products with this dual character. Specifically, Marx claims that labour must be considered both as 'concrete labour' and 'abstract labour'. Concrete labour creates use-values; it is labour of a particular type and purpose, creating goods of a particular type and purpose. Abstract labour creates exchange value. It has one pertinent feature only: its duration. The only pertinent feature of the object it creates is its price. Thus, under capitalism, labour is simultaneously both abstract and concrete, and its product is both a use-value and an exchange value. In a letter to Engels in 1867, Marx said that the account of the 'twofold character of labour' is one of 'the best points in my book' (M. 564).

Why should this be so important? The point, perhaps only implicit in *Capital*, is that the twofold character of labour introduces a possible conflict or division within capitalist production. In producing a use-value, one wants to produce an object that fits its purposes well. A shirt should be comfortable, well-fitting, long-lasting and so on. Yet from the point of view of exchange value all that matters is what it costs, and that similar products can continue to be sold in the future. So it is important to make shirts that don't last too long. Production must serve two purposes: the creation of use-value and the continuing creation of exchange value.

The requirements of the latter may compromise the former, frustrating our natures as productive beings (another form of alienation).

This, then, was the first of Marx's major insights into capitalist economics. The second concerns exchange value alone; in particular, the question of how it is possible for a capitalist to make a profit. Well, we would all like to know the answer to that, although in one way it is very straightforward: buy cheap, sell expensive (if you can). But this is not enough to explain how it is possible for capitalists in general to make a profit. That is, how can the whole capitalist economy return a profit year after year? This is the question that, according to Engels in his speech at Marx's graveside, had baffled all previous economists.

To bring out the problem, consider the contrast between two types of economy, both of which involve the production of goods and their exchange. In the first, relatively undeveloped, economy, individuals produce goods, or, as Marx calls them, commodities, then sell them to get the money to purchase the commodities they want or need. A cobbler may make shoes, and then sell them to acquire the money to buy food and clothes. Marx represents this as the 'circuit of commodities':

C–M–C

C here stands for commodity, and M for money. The worker makes a commodity, sells it for money and then buys and consumes other commodities. End of story.

Now consider the behaviour of the industrial capitalist. He or she buys commodities of various sorts. These tend to fall into the categories of labour, plant, and raw materials. These, in combination, produce a new commodity, which is then sold. But clearly there would be no point in going to all this trouble unless the money received at the end of the cycle is greater than the money advanced at the start. Thus Marx also presents what he calls the 'circuit of capital'.

M–C–M′

Here M is the money advanced, C the commodities purchased, transformed, then sold, and M′ the increased amount of money received when the produced goods are sold. Money advanced for the sake of making a profit is called 'capital' (hence 'capitalism'). The purest form of this is banking, which develops the short and sweet cycle:

M–M′

Money is advanced purely with the intention of getting an increased sum back, without dirtying one's hands with production or sales along the way.

Now, in M–C–M′, which, for Marx, is the paradigm of capitalist production, the capitalist makes a profit. Marx's question is this: how is it possible if everything exchanges at its value? That is, we know how to make a profit, if we are lucky, in a market of changing prices. But if prices remain constant, where does profit come from? How does it even get into the equation? We must, I think, confess that this is a puzzle. We are so used, now, to the idea that somehow capitalism makes positive profits year after year, that 'investments' somehow naturally bring 'return', that we forget to ask: where does this come from?

Marx wants us to be properly impressed with this difficulty, for he takes himself to be the first person in the history of economic thought to have been able to solve it, and spends many pages exploring dead-end solutions. Finally he lets us into the secret. There must be, he says, a commodity which creates more value in its use than it cost. And, he tells us, there is a very special commodity just of this kind: labour power. Suppose I, Moneybags, the capitalist, hire a worker for a day, thus purchasing 'a day's labour power'. How much should it cost me? Now schooled, at least from the business pages, in elementary economic theory, you might start talking about supply and demand; how skilled the job is; how scarce the talent needed to do it; and, perhaps, how unpleasant the task and so on. But for Marx all of this is superficial and the price of labour is ultimately determined in the same way as the price of any other commodity. That is, by the quantity of socially necessary labour power required for its production.

This may seem a strange idea. What is the time it takes to produce a day's labour power? Well, it is the time it takes to produce the commodities necessary to sustain the worker for the day. Not only food, but a contribution to the cost of housing, clothes, and so on. (In some formulations Marx also talks of sustaining the worker's family too, but we can leave this complication to one side.) Furthermore, highly trained workers cost more to produce than ordinary ones, and this is why, according on Marx's analysis, they cost more. The cost of training is spread out in their products over an entire working life.

For Marx, then, labour power is a commodity like any other. It can be bought and sold on the market at its value. So, to adopt one of the simple models so beloved of economists, let us suppose that a worker needs a basket of commodities in order to survive, and that the commodities in the basket contain a grand total of four hours of other people's labour (i.e. these commodities took four hours to produce when everything is added up). The price of the worker then, for the day, will be the cost of the commodities in the basket. In other words a day's wages will be the amount of money sufficient to produce these goods. To create equivalent value the worker must work four hours. This is known as 'necessary labour' (not to be confused with the concept of 'socially necessary labour' introduced earlier). It is in effect what the worker needs to do to create the value of his or her wages. In this example, we said, that amounted to four hours.

But, of course, Moneybags is hardly going to let the worker return home after completing four hours' labour. On the contrary, having paid for a whole day's labour, a whole day's labour is expected. Let us suppose, in these relatively humane times, a day's labour standardly lasts eight hours (Marx, himself, was more familiar with a workers who performed an average of eleven hours a day, six days a week). We have heard that the first four hours, which create the value to pay wages, is known as necessary labour. The further four hours is *surplus* labour. Surplus labour creates surplus value, and on Marx's analysis, surplus value is the source of all profit. It is this that makes the difference between the money advanced and the money received. The process of 'extracting' surplus value is called 'exploitation'. Finally we have arrived at the point of Marx's great discovery. Under capitalism all profit is ultimately the result of the exploitation of the workers. For, by this account, there is simply nowhere else for profit to come from.

Now you may think, either this represents the workers as very stupid, or there must be something wrong with Marx's analysis. For if workers posses this incredibly valuable thing—labour power—why don't they keep it to themselves, or, at least sell it for a decent price?

The reason why they don't keep it to themselves and thus harness its full earning potential, says Marx, is that they can't. According to Marx one of the conditions of capitalism's existence is that there must be a class of workers who are free in an ironic 'double sense'. First, they must be free from feudal ties, which would otherwise prevent them from entering any sort of market transaction. Second, they must be 'free' from independent access to the means of production. In other words they must both be able to work for capitalists and need to. They acquiesce in their own exploitation only because they have no alternative. They cannot work for themselves as they have nothing to work on or with, no land or other resources. Thus they must hire out their labour power to the highest bidder.

This is nicely illustrated in Marx's tale of 'unhappy Mr Peel':

A Mr Peel . . . took with him from England to the Swan River district of Western Australia means of subsistence and of production to the amount of £50,000. This Mr Peel even had the foresight to bring besides 3,000 persons of the working class, men, women, and children. Once he arrived at his destination, Mr Peel was left without a servant to make his bed or fetch him water from the river. Unhappy Mr Peel, who provided for everything except the export of English relations of production to Swan River. (*Capital* 933)

In other words, rational individuals who can acquire land for themselves, as they could at that time in Western Australia, are very likely to choose to do this rather than selling their labour power to the capitalists. So, in general, Marx thinks that the worker sells his or her labour power only because there is no real option.

Nevertheless, even though they must sell their labour power, why so cheap? After all it is a commodity of special value, the only thing on the market capable of making a profit. And, it seems, potentially a very nice profit too. Wouldn't this mean that capitalists in competition with each other would try to get as much of it as possible? And wouldn't such competition drive up the price, thus giving the workers an increasingly decent wage?

This argument seems no more than a simple application of the laws of supply and demand. If labour is regarded as valuable it will be greatly in demand and so the price will rise. If the supply of labour is fixed, as it appears to be—there are, after all, no 'labour factories'—then it will be very scarce and the price must rise, even to the point where no profit can be made, according to pure theory. So, some have argued, Marx is quite mistaken. Rather than being a universal feature of capitalism, in a properly functioning free market exploitation cannot even exist.

Earlier socialists, convinced that exploitation must exist, yet aware of the theory of supply and demand, tried to grapple with the same, inconvenient, problem. Now, if the supply of labour could, somehow, increase in response to increasing demand, this would help keep wages down, and thus rescue the argument that capitalism is exploitative of the workers. Accordingly some socialists noted that as wages rise the standard of living will rise too. This will encourage workers to have more children, increasing the labour supply. This, then, renders labour less scarce and wages should fall back again.

Ingenious though this may be, unfortunately it has a couple of flaws. First, there is simply no evidence that rising standards of living lead people to have more children. If anything the reverse seems to be true. Second, even if there were such a trend it would take children too long to reach the labour force—in Marx's day at least six years! Even this is too slow to exert the required downward pressure on wages.

Marx's own solution also concentrates on the supply of labour, but in a very different way. It starts by considering the behaviour of an individual capitalist as wages tend to rise. The rise in wages will affect profitability, and so the capitalist will become increasingly desperate to take whatever steps are most likely to restore profits, and, if possible, keep the edge against competitors.

When wages are low it can be rational to employ people even when machinery is available to perform the same task. Many people will have seen photographs of labourers in India, sitting by the side of the road hand-crushing stones into gravel, to make ballast for building. A machine could perform the labour of hundreds. But if wages are very low and machines expensive, why use machines? However as wage costs rise what was uneconomic may become economic, and the capitalist may start to look for labour-saving machinery. A powerful Marxist image is that of labourers whose final task is to make the machines that will replace them.

Now, what is rational for one capitalist is likely to be rational for others too, and, in the face of rising wages, there will be a general movement to cut labour costs by purchasing labour-saving machinery. Each capitalist acts alone, in pursuit of his or her personal profit. But each capitalist is likely to act in exactly the same way, inadvertently creating a quite unintended, but very satisfactory consequence for the capitalists. As workers are replaced by machines, and, thus, fired as no longer needed, this restocks what Marx calls the 'Industrial Reserve Army of the Unemployed'. Remember that wages were rising because labour is scarce. Well, in response each capitalist takes special measures, which happens to lead to the mass redundancy of workers, so that labour is no longer scarce. Therefore wages, which rose because of labour shortage, will fall back again. The capitalist wins twice over. Less labour is needed, and now it can be paid less. Marx argues that wages will fall back to their values: essentially a subsistence wage.

The account of the 'employment cycle' is worth thinking about. Marx's theory is that the Industrial Reserve Army of the Unemployed is essential to the functioning of capitalism. It acts as a 'dead-weight' to the aspirations of those in employment. Their wages will always be held down for as long as others want their jobs. In 'boom' times, the Industrial Reserve Army becomes depleted, and wages can rise above their values. But the good times cannot last, and mechanisms exist, as we have seen, to bring wages back down.

This analysis is enormously significant. First, it involves the claim that capitalism, as part of its natural functioning, involves an employment cycle. There is no tendency to equilibrium, either in the short term or long term. Rather the economy has to be understood in dynamic terms, as going through regular cycles. Consequently the politician's Holy Grail of permanent full employment is a mirage. As we have seen, on Marx's analysis anything close to full employment will be a short-term phenomenon. Defences against rising wages see to that.

Second we should note that workers are also consumers. When they are relatively well off they will buy more, fuelling a boom, but when unemployed their purchasing power virtually disappears. So capitalists will see their sales fall, leading to unsold stocks, and in some cases pushing them over the brink to ruin. 'In these crises there breaks out an epidemic that, in all earlier epochs would have seemed an absurdity—the epidemic of over-production' (*Communist Manifesto* M. 250).

In other words, along with the employment cycle goes the

trade cycle of boom and bust. This cycle, brought to Marx's attention by Engels in 1843, has been the bugbear of economics ever since. No economist has ever worked out a way of eliminating the destructive cycle of boom and recession. Of course, they have found ways of mitigating its effects— contrary to Marx's expectation that it would get worse and worse—but they can do nothing to eliminate it entirely. If Marx is right this is only to be expected.

Finally it is worth commenting on a humanist plea, beloved of the sort of people who write 'why, oh why?' letters to newspapers. In times of high unemployment it is also common to find people working long hours, or, at least, longer than they would prefer. Suppose we have 10 per cent unemployment and a 40-hour week. Time and time again it is discovered that, if only we were to cut the working week by the right proportion, we could eliminate unemployment. So why don't we do this?

One answer is that, in a capitalist economy, there is no one in charge to bring this about. But Marx's more theoretical answer would be that the proposal is, in any case, impossible. Eliminating unemployment means that the capitalist cannot meaningfully threaten the worker with the sack. It thus eliminates the capitalist's bargaining advantage, and so would inevitably lead to rising wages and improving working conditions. While a marked improvement for the worker, this would be a disaster for the capitalist, who would start looking for labour saving machinery again. So the whole filthy business starts again.

The moral of the story is that capitalism needs unemployment in order to be profitable. And it contains mechanisms that will achieve this. No amount of letter writing to the newspapers will make any difference, or even following the instructions in the letters. If we were to have an economy of permanent full employment it would not be capitalism.

Now, it might be objected that there is something very puzzling indeed about all this. If all profit comes from labour shouldn't it be quite irrational for a capitalist to lay off workers and replace them with machines. Wouldn't this be a way of reducing profits rather than increasing them?

Marx's answer to this is: yes and no. Consider the behaviour of an individual capitalist. This person buys commodities to allow production to take place. These constitute the costs of production, and the capitalist calculates profits as a percentage of all costs, whether the money is spent on wages, machinery, raw materials, power or whatever. No capitalist calculates with the Labour Theory of Value in mind, assuming that profit only comes from labour. Consequently a saving is a saving, wherever it comes from, and potentially can add to profits. Provided that revenues remain steady any reduction in costs means a rise in profits.

So, it seems, capitalists can increase their profits by cutting their labour force, provided that they buy labour-saving machinery. But isn't this to concede that Marx must be wrong in believing that labour is the source of all profit? Not so fast! Marx's argument is that while labour is the source of all profit in the economy as a whole, where that profit is created may not be where it is reaped. And we should see the sense in this. Otherwise it would follow that labour-intensive industries, such as hand-made lace, would be incredibly profitable, whereas highly mechanized industries, such as oil refining, would be barely profitable at all. Consequently we need to think on an economy-wide basis. While an individual capitalist may be able to increase his or her profits by cutting labour, ultimately other capitalists will suffer. There will be less total profit in the economy, even though our hero, who has just laid off some workers, and now has a lean, slim labour force, will be able to get a larger share of it, or at least until the competition catches up.

This is an example of the classic structure in game theory known as the multi-person Prisoners' Dilemma. What is perfectly rational for a given person, taken individually, can be a disaster for the collective as a whole when it represents a general pattern of behaviour. This is a very common problem, and is the reason, for example that left to themselves fishermen will in some cases overfish stocks to the point of extinction. It is rational for any individual fisherman to try to increase yields as much as possible, even in the face of falling catches. But if everyone does this we fall into a spiral of decline. It remains individually rational to catch as many fish as possible, but collectively terrible when everyone does this.

On this analysis the capitalists are in a similar dilemma. Each wants to increase profits, and with wages rising must cut labour costs. But when everyone does this it means that the proportion of money spent on labour costs is reduced. This, in turn, means that the rate of profit in the economy will fall. And this, indeed, is what Marx predicts. As more and more is spent on increasingly advanced machinery, and, as a proportion, less on labour, we can, in general, expect the rate of profit to fall. Of course there are many further complications, but this, at least, is at the heart of Marx's supposed 'law of the falling rate of profit'. Marx appears to argue that over time the rate of profit under capitalism will fall . . . and fall . . . and fall. (Is he right in this prediction? It turns out that the rate of profit is actually a very hard thing to measure, and there seems little undisputed evidence one way or the other.)

We have seen two complementary threats to capitalism. In addition to the falling rate of profit we have seen Marx's analysis of the boom/bust cycle. Capitalist crisis will follow capitalist crisis, and with the increasing globalization of trade, and growing commodification of all activities, each one will be more damaging than its predecessor. In sum, then, the natural functioning of capitalism means that it is a system in terminal decline; like so many of its products it has built-in obsolescence. Eventually it becomes so weak that it will be vulnerable to revolutionary overthrow.

Recall that we began examining Marx's economic theory as an adjunct to his theory of history. Just as feudalism was taken over by capitalism, capitalism will be replaced by communism. We have seen, now, why Marx thinks that capitalism will come to end. At the highest level of abstraction it fails because eventually it will fetter the development of the productive forces. In more detail the falling rate of profit and increasing tendency to crisis does the harm. But why is any of this a reason for thinking that communism will come on the scene? That is our next topic.

The transition to communism

The twentieth century witnessed a number of 'Marxist' revolutions. Those in Russia and China are, no doubt, the most significant, but there were, of course, many others. Let us, for the moment, consider the Russian revolution.

Coming out of the nineteenth century, and into the First World War, Russia was in a sorry state indeed. The peasants revolutionary slogan 'bread, land, and peace' (a reasonable enough request, on the face of it) summed up their plight perfectly. Economically Russia was very backward compared to the major powers of Europe. A common estimate is that it was around fifty years behind. Consequently, particularly in time of war, it had a desperate, and failing, struggle even to feed its people.

The demand for land reflects the fact that Russia was still, essentially, a feudal economy, with the land under the control of the local aristocracy. The peasantry didn't demand so much as a vote, or a say in general politics, but enough land to feed themselves. In effect they wanted to break the stranglehold of the aristocratic landlords.

The plea for peace needs little comment. Drawn into a world war of which, perhaps, it had little understanding, Russia's youth was being slaughtered as the Germans advanced. Who wouldn't demand peace?

This powerful cocktail of extreme discontent provided an opportunity for the small but highly active Marxist movement. A revolution broke out in February 1917, and a provisional, social democratic, government was put in place.

However, the Germans, hoping that the revolutionaries would take Russia out of the war, were keen to offer their encouragement, and Lenin was whisked from exile in Zurich, in a notorious 'sealed-train' through Germany to Petrograd (later renamed Leningrad). That is, one carriage of the train was kept firmly locked so that Lenin could not disembark in Germany and stir up the workers there. Within a few months of his arrival in Russia, in combination with Trotsky and others, Lenin succeeded in organizing the overthrow of the provisional government, gaining power for the Bolsheviks (we will here more of these shortly) in October. The peasants' demands for land, bread, and peace were initially addressed by means of a highly concessive peace treaty with the Germans (the Treaty of Brest–Litovsk), and the redistribution of the landed estates. Perhaps inevitably a civil war, of an exceptionally brutal nature, ensued, in which the Bolsheviks eventually consolidated their rule, though at enormous cost, and whether the peasants really did get what they wanted is a good question.

Rather than answer it, we should look at some of the general features of this revolution. First, before the revolution Russia was, as we said, essentially a feudal economy, only just beginning, belatedly, to transform itself into capitalism. Thus its people suffered the 'double-oppression' of feudal land laws and the beginnings of capitalist working conditions. The revolutionaries grasped political power when the opportunity arose, and used this to attempt to impose a communist economy. So, we may ask, how does this all fit in with the theory of historical materialism?

The answer is that in terms of pure Marxist theory (as distinct from later 'Marxist/Leninism') it appears to fit very badly indeed. Marx predicted that the communist revolution would take place in the most advanced capitalist systems. Such systems would have developed the productive forces— technology—to the highest point that capitalism is capable of, and then, through their own internal crises, give way. Russia had barely entered a capitalist phase, and no one could pretend that it had developed high productive capabilities.

This gave rise to trenchant debate within the Russian revolutionary movement. One group—known as Mensheviks— argued that the conditions in Russia were not ripe for a Marxist revolution. Any attempt, they believed, would lead to disaster. The Bolsheviks ridiculed the 'doctrinaire dogmas' of the Mensheviks and argued that the revolutionaries should seize the opportunity that they had in front of them, which may not come again. The Mensheviks were memorably dismissed by the Bolshevik (formerly a Menshevik) Trotsky (as he himself reports in his *History of the Russian Revolution* Volume 3): 'You are pitiful isolated individuals; your role is played out. Go where you belong from now on—to the dustbin of history.' Nevertheless, the Mensheviks may have been the more faithful followers of Marx. Certainly this was the view of the Socialist Party of Great Britain, who now boast that they condemned the Russian revolution as 'non-Marxist' within its first 24 hours.

So the Russian revolution is an object lesson in 'how not to have a Marxist revolution'. But how are you meant to do it? First of all, according to Marxist theory the first country to achieve revolution to communism should have been Britain, or some other highly developed industrial economy (although Marx did suggest it might break out first in the less-developed economy of Germany). Once communism had taken root elsewhere Russian communism could catch a lift on their beneficent shirt-tails, but Russia was far too backwards to be a pioneer.

Classic Marxist theory suggests that the capitalist economy must have developed to a certain point in order to make revolution a real possibility. Marx often talks about the material conditions of communism 'developing in the womb of the old society' (*1859 Preface*, M. 426), and, in a somewhat incongruous image, capitalism developing 'its own grave-diggers' (*Communist Manifesto*, M. 255). The two come together when we realize that, gruesomely, capitalism dies in childbirth.

We have already seen one absolutely key feature. The forces of production—technology—must have developed to a high degree. One reason for this is that communist society requires 'abundance'. Now, it is not entirely clear what this means. On the most utopian reading, it means that under communism anyone can have whatever they desire, however frivolous, without this having any effect whatsoever on what anyone else can have. A more moderate understanding is that there will be sufficient availability of goods so that all are able to lead a 'flourishing' life, and that their reasonable needs can be satisfied.

The reason for this requirement is related to Marx's understanding of class, and, in particular, the reason why class exists. Marx suggests that social classes do not develop until there is a possibility of productive surplus; that is, not until an individual human being, on average, can produce more than he or she needs in order to survive. Once surplus is possible, this also opens up the possibility of one group, or class, living off the work of another class. Now the more productive society becomes, the greater the potential surplus, and the bigger and richer the exploiting class can become. Under capitalism one class lives a relatively leisured, potentially fulfilling, life, with the opportunity to pursue education, art, literature, and culture (whether or not they decide to avail themselves of this opportunity), while another class struggles to feed and clothe itself. However, once society becomes sufficiently productive it becomes, in theory, possible for everyone in society to lead a life finally worthy of human beings. Free from need, people can develop their individual potential.

Now, to be clear, Marx is not saying that having reached such a level of productivity classes will disappear and exploitation end, for it is perfectly possible that the super-rich will do everything they can to cream off the surplus and preserve their privilege. But rather his point is that abundance makes the end of class-divided society a real possibility. Without abundance class division is bound to reappear, as different groups fight to control the surplus. This was one of the particularly unattractive features of Soviet communism, in which party officials grasped privileges that were not available to the general citizens.

So the argument seems to be that high productive power is

necessary to create abundance, without which we will never transcend class-divided society. As capitalism develops the productive forces it also, therefore, develops one of the necessary conditions to allow for its eventual replacement. We have also seen that the revolution will not take place until this growth is fettered by the economic structure. Just as feudalism fettered the development of the productive forces as it had no incentive to introduce the division of labour, capitalism too must fetter this development before we enter a period of revolution. In this case, though, the fettering takes a somewhat different form, in the shape of the capitalist boom/bust cycle and an ever-falling rate of profit. The worsening and deepening of regular crises, together with reduction in profit, will lead eventually to a stagnating economy and a revolutionary proletariat who 'have nothing to lose but their chains' (*Communist Manifesto*, M. 271).

But this is still not yet the whole story. For elements of communism are developing under capitalism, behind our backs. Engels, in particular, points out that a number of elements of advanced capitalism are either already models of communism, or ripe for take-over.

Take, for example, the joint-stock company. This is the familiar large organization which is owned by its shareholders, which might, today, number millions of people, especially when one realizes how much is currently held by pension funds, for the benefit of their members. Now, one of the old arguments against communism is that people will only act in an efficient and productive way if they seek their own profit. People need incentives to work hard, to

chase down market opportunities, or to close down unprofit-
able lines of business, but the only incentive that works is
personal profit, so it is said. Thus, the argument goes, only
capitalism will be efficient because only capitalism gives individuals the right incentives. However, according to Marx and
Engels, the existence and success of the joint-stock company
shows that this argument is mistaken. Even by the 1860s the
image of the lone, entrepreneurial capitalist, acting as an
individual hero of enterprise, was already a rarity. Companies
were owned by a raft of shareholders, but managed very
effectively by salaried employees. This, then, is the point. The
joint-stock company shows that it is perfectly common under
capitalism for some individuals to manage an organization
for the benefit of a large number of strangers. In effect this is
all communism asks of people, yet it already happens under
capitalism.

Now, of course, under capitalism managers have all man-
ner of financial and personal incentives. They seek pay rises,
promotions, bonuses, share options, and the like. But their
fate is ultimately decided by the shareholders. They know
that the major fruits of their endeavour will be the shareholders' dividend, not personal profit. The central difference between the capitalist firm and communist economies
is that under communism, in effect, everyone will be an equal
shareholder. But here we see capitalism already evolving
communist-like structures.

Another example of an element of communism existing
under capitalism is large-scale industrial production. Here
we can have perhaps thousands of people co-operating

together in production. In effect, Marx says, production under capitalism is already 'socialized'. So this shows that human beings are indeed capable of very elaborate co-ordinated action; again one of the prerequisites of communism.

Furthermore, capitalism contains many activities which are already state owned or organized in such a way that it would be easy for the state to take over. Examples of the former include companies that provide for communication— especially the post office—utility companies and other nationalized industries. Marx and Engels predicted that as capitalist firms got bigger by beating off the competition or merging, and thus came to have a monopoly position in their industry, governments would be obliged to take them into public ownership to prevent them abusing their market power. (In fact, this menace has been dealt with in other ways; through breaking up very large concerns, or through the creation of industry regulators.) Other firms which, although not monopolies, would be ripe for take-over by the state, include the banks and other financial institutions. So yet again here is something growing within capitalism that could easily be turned to communist advantage.

Now, all these points—the possibility of abundance; the fettering of the development of the productive forces; the development of communist-friendly structures may be very suggestive, but still, how exactly is the revolution to take place?

Unfortunately Marx was never as explicit about this as one might hope, but we should briefly explore two different models both of which are indicated at points within his works. One is what I shall call the 'economics first' model; the second is the 'politics first' model.

The idea of the economics first model is that just as feudal economics gave way to capitalist economics long before feudal politics was overturned, capitalist economics would fall to communist economics, before the communist political revolution. Here is one way of developing this idea. At a time of capitalist crisis unemployed workers could pool their meagre resources to set up co-operative enterprises of their own. Working conditions would be reasonably decent, for the workers would not impose terrible conditions on themselves. Wages could also be higher than elsewhere in the economy as the bloodsucking, parasitic capitalist is not there demanding his piece of the action. Prices of goods might also be reasonable as the workers would be selling to themselves, or, at least, people like them. Co-operatives would share knowledge with other enterprises as they need not see them as competitors, to everyone's benefit.

In this fantasy, the co-operative movement ever grows in strength, just at the time that capitalism is at its weakest. One can just about imagine workers abandoning capitalist enterprises to join in the co-operative sector of the economy, eventually to a point where capitalism begins to be a marginal part of the economy. Co-operatives would merge or form associations, coming to dominate the economy as a whole. At this point the economic revolution has already taken place, and it would only be a matter of time before a political revolution occurs to oust the last vestiges of the capitalist class from political control. Then the revolution is complete.

Now, I should admit at once that there is no evidence that this is how Marx and Engels thought that the revolution to communism would take place. Rather it is what one would expect if the transition from capitalism to communism is to happen in the way in which the transition from feudalism to capitalism is said by Marx and Engels to have taken place; that is, if the same model is to apply to all revolutionary transformations of society. On this account, communism comes into existence as part of a natural evolution, without necessarily being the conscious aim of anyone, or, at least, not until very late in the process.

The alternative, I said, is the 'politics first' model. This is very much more familiar. The thought is simply that, when capitalism is fatally weakened through the declining rate of profit, ever-deepening crisis, and so on, the growing revolutionary movement takes its opportunity, and grasps political power. Once in power the proletariat transforms the economy, which is a relatively straightforward task, given that capitalism has developed the 'communist-friendly' structures already described. And there is no doubt that the politics first model is the 'official' Marxist account of communist revolution. It is very clearly indicated in the *Communist Manifesto*, for example, although this may be because Marx thought that the revolution was actually in process as he was writing it. In either case, though, it is absolutely essential that, at the time of revolution, the productive forces are highly developed, yet fettered. It is equally imperative that capitalism has already developed in its womb significant elements of communism. On the politics first model we also need a large, active, revolutionary mass movement to have formed. But either way we can safely conclude that the world has not (yet?) seen a Marxist revolution.

The nature of communism

How would communism be organized? This was one of the questions that gripped the group that has subsequently become known as the 'First International': The International Working Men's Association, founded in 1864, a remarkable association. It contained the leading radical and revolutionary figures of day, including Marx and Engels, of course, and was dedicated to the revolutionary overthrow of existing society. Setting the pattern for future groups of a similar nature, it eventually broke up as a result of bitter internal division.

One important dispute revolved around Marx and the leading anarchist Bakunin. Marx had argued that after the revolution there must be a period of 'dictatorship of the proletariat' in order to expunge from society those still existing elements of the capitalist economy. But sooner or later this revolutionary state would 'wither away'. Bakunin countered that once it had its dictatorship the proletariat would never let go. The dictatorship of the proletariat may not be all that much of an improvement over the dictatorship of the bourgeoisie.

Bakunin, was treated with utter contempt by Marx, who, in a letter of 1871 to an associate, accused him of being 'a man devoid of all theoretical knowledge' (M. 636), who 'does not understand a thing about social revolution' (from Marx's notes on Bakunin's *Statism and Anarchy*, M. 607). In retrospect, however, Bakunin appears remarkably prescient. Indeed his argument is exactly the theme of George Orwell's satire of Soviet communism, *Animal Farm*. Of course, one has to add that Bakunin's own proposals for anarchist society remain, thankfully, untested, and, as we saw, Soviet communism is not a good model for how Marx thought his ideas should be implemented. But we are still left with our question: what did Marx say about the arrangement of communism, beyond the point that there would be a period of the dictatorship of the proletariat?

Despite the voluminous quantity of Marx's work as a whole, it contains very little about the nature of communism. Part of this reticence comes from Marx's contention that it is not for him to draw up 'recipes for the cookshops of the future' (*Capital* 99). That is, he suggests that the movement to communism must follow its own lines of development, and is a real historical movement, not the implementation of an idea or principle (M. 256). As Marx puts the point in *The German Ideology*:

> Communism is not for us a state of affairs which is to be established, or an ideal to which reality will have to adjust itself. We call communism the real movement which abolishes the present state of things. (M. 187)

Thus we must see where history leads us. It would be as absurd for Marx to draw up a blueprint of communism as it would have been for a fifteenth-century scholar to attempt to provide the details of a capitalist system.

Sane though this may sound, it probably does not have a very powerful motivating force. 'Let us see where history takes us' is not a strong political rallying cry. It is hard to see how it could be rational to take on the risk of a revolution without some pretty determinate aims. But, of course, Marx does leave many clues about his expectations for communism. Many of these arise in his criticisms of capitalism.

From his Early Writings we know that one of the chief defects of capitalism is that it is alienating. Thus we would expect communism not to be alienating; it is a society in which man is not fragmented, not dominated by alien forces, not subjugated. From the theory of history we know that communism is expected to be a realm of some abundance, and that this is possible only when we have reached a high level of productive power.

What else? We also know that many of capitalism's problems, according to Marx, stem from its 'anarchic' nature, and that there are strong indications that some sort of rational, planned, organization is the solution. But beyond this there is not much to go on. In a notorious passage in *The German Ideology*, yet another work Marx left unpublished, he writes:

> In communist society, where nobody has one exclusive sphere of activity but each can become accomplished in any

branch he wishes, society regulates the general production, and thus makes it possible for me to do one thing today and another tomorrow, to hunt in the morning, fish in the afternoon, rear cattle in the evening, criticize after dinner, just as I have a mind, without ever becoming hunter, fisherman, cowherd, or critic. (M. 185)

Finally, there is Marx's late, and very angry, *Critique of the Gotha Programme*. This was written in 1875, in a rage at the proposals that had been put forward following a conference the purpose of which was to unify two strands in the German worker's movement. Marx felt that too much of the programme represented the erroneous views of the other party, followers of the recently deceased Ferdinand Lassalle. The Gotha Programme's failure to take the true path prompted Marx to new heights of pedantry in criticism, and here he is much more explicit about certain of his views than elsewhere. In particular it is here that Marx sets out his view that communist society would 'inscribe on its banners: from each according to his ability; to each according to his need' (M. 615).

How consistent a picture can we gain from these various strands? Let us consider three topics: the nature of work; of economic organization; and of distribution of material resources.

As we saw, the hope that work should be non-alienating comes out of the criticisms of the capitalist system. And what better sketch of a non-alienated society than one where one can work at whatever type of activity one wishes? Indeed, under such conditions work may well be 'life's prime want', as Marx also says in the *Critique of the Gotha Programme*. This ideal combines beautifully with Marx's notion that product-ive activity—labour—is man's most distinctive and essential quality.

Yet we also have to recognize that the idea that: 'society will be re-organized so that work will be life's prime want' also has its defects as a revolutionary call to arms. How many of the exploited, alienated proletariat would sign up to that? In a more pragmatic mode, Engels argued that the chief attrac-tion of communism is that it would be so well-organized that there would be much less work to be done (and more people to do it: the army the clergy and swindling middlemen could all turn to honest labour). This, at least, is what he said in his speeches to the workers.

But the central difficulty, of course, is how work can be both non-alienating and highly productive. High productiv-ity appears to depend on a developed division of labour, and it is this more than anything else which leads to alienated labour. Hunting whenever you feel in the mood, just won't do it. High productivity seems to bring alienation in its train.

Furthermore, although Marx claims that communism will awaken new creative powers in all of us, this does not address the question of how we can deal with mundane work. One answer is that anything that can be mechanized will be (including maintenance of the machines?), which will leave us time to pursue fulfilling occupations, through both work and leisure. This, indeed, is suggested by Marx in a famous passage from *Capital* Volume 3:

Just as the savage must wrestle with Nature to satisfy his wants, to maintain and reproduce life, so must civilised man, and he must do so in all social formations and under all possible modes of production. With his development this realm of physical necessity expands as a result of his wants; but, at the same time, the forces of production which satisfy these wants also increase. Freedom in this field can only consist in socialized man, the associated producers, rationally regulating their interchange with Nature, bringing it under their common control, instead of being ruled by it as by the blind forces of Nature; and achieving this with the least expenditure of energy and under conditions most favourable to, and worthy of, their human nature. But it nonetheless still remains a realm of necessity. Beyond it begins that development of human energy which is an end in itself, the true realm of freedom, which, however, can blossom forth only with this realm of necessity as its basis. The shortening of the working-day is its basic prerequisite. (M. 534–5)

Whether or not this is a real practical possibility, it at least seems a coherent, attractive, ideal.

We also see a possible difficulty in Marx's reflections about overall economic organization. On the one hand, I can turn to whatever I want 'just as I have a mind'; on the other the problem with capitalism was the anarchy of production, to be replaced by rational planning. But Marx's own suggestion here looks more anarchic than planned, even though, as he says 'society regulates the general production'. Perhaps we shouldn't take the 'hunting and fishing' passage too seriously. It was, after all, in a relatively early text that was unpublished in Marx's lifetime and never repeated.

Finally, a quick word about distribution. How should goods be allocated to individuals? Marx's dictum that each would contribute according to their ability, but receive according to need obviously anticipates a world in which everyone willingly pulls their weight—they do what they can. They do not raise questions about the return they are getting for their labour, or try to ensure some proportionality between input and output. Utopian? But this is how the family often works. You contribute what you reasonably can, and your needs are taken care of as far as this is possible.

The crunch question, of course, is what about those who refuse to contribute? If they fail to contribute according to ability, will communist society refuse them what they need? Marx does not discuss this, but I think that his official answer is that this question would not arise. Once labour is 'life's prime want' who would refuse to work if they could? But the point can be pressed. Suppose there are people who just refuse to play the game. Presumably Marx should say that communist society would have to find a way of dealing with this issue, if it does arise, but it is not for him, from the standpoint of capitalist society, to tell them what to do.

So, imagine we could reach something like Marx's goal. Most of production is mechanized, but the work remaining for individuals to do is highly fulfilling. Accordingly the distinction between work and leisure is erased, and people exercise and enjoy their creativity in ever-new ways. Each has their needs satisfied, and, indeed, wants for nothing. It is the end of strife and conflict, and a fitting world, at last, for human beings. It sounds wonderful, of course, but could things really be like this? We will look at this question shortly.

3

Assessment

Introduction

Having now understood the main lines of Marx's thought, we can finally begin to answer our opening question: what is alive and what is dead?

Now, before sifting through the ideas one by one it is worth emphasizing that there is an important sense in which all of Marx's thought is still alive. Each one of Marx's major ideas is still very much worth studying. One reason for this is the history of the twentieth century. Marx's influence, in both theory and practice, is beyond measure. There are so many aspects of the current world, and current world of ideas, that we would simply be unable to grasp without an appreciation of at least the bold outlines of Marx's thought. This alone would be enough to justify close attention. But there is much more to it than this, although perhaps it is not quite so easy to convey. Consider the great philosophers: Plato, Aristotle, Descartes, Locke, Hume, and Kant, for example. If we were not to think these figures were worth reading, then who would be? But why do we read them? Is it because they have proved, or established any firm results? In the words of the late Berton Dreben, a Harvard philosopher of great influence though very few published writings, 'Think of Leibniz. Perhaps the most intelligent man who every lived. But how much of his philosophical writing was true? How much *even makes sense?*' Dreben went on to describe Hegel's *Phenomenology of Spirit* as 'perhaps both man's greatest achievement and man's greatest folly'.

My point is that we value the work of the greatest philosophers for their power, rigour, depth, inventiveness, insight, originality, systematic vision, and, no doubt, other virtues too. Truth, or at least the whole truth and nothing but the truth, seems way down the list. Now, we have to be careful here. The works of the great philosophers could have been created only if their authors passionately believed that they had just discovered the truth, or were on the verge of doing so. Single-minded pursuit of the truth is at the centre of all great philosophy. Yet the value of the resulting works does not depend on its having actually achieved this goal. To put it bluntly there are things much more interesting than truth. Understood this way, Marx's works are as alive as anyone's.

On the other hand Marx gave up philosophy early in his life, and thought of himself much more as a scientist. While a scientific theory known to be false can be of great interest to historians of ideas, it is not much use to a scientist. On this account truth takes centre stage again. So what I shall now do is take in turn each of the Early Writings, the theory of history, and economics. I won't do anything quite as crude as listing what is true and false in each, but I will assess them in a number of ways. Some elements will be criticized for their vagueness, or the fact that Marx failed to substantiate them (they don't follow from other things he said, and from which he thought they followed). Others will be highlighted for their insight and the contribution they made to our understanding of the world. On this level, then, we uncover a final set of reasons for still reading Marx today.

Early Writings

Although the exposition of Marx's Early Writings was fairly lengthy, in assessment we can be relatively brief. The topics we discussed included religion; the philosophy of historical materialism; alienation, including alienated labour; money and credit; liberalism; and emancipation. For myself I find Marx's remarks on most of these issues full of insight. This is not to say, of course, that I am ready to swallow them whole, and considerable questions can be raised. First I shall point to a few of the difficulties that I find in this part of Marx's work.

Marx's analysis of religion can be broken into four parts. First, human beings create God in their own image (Feuerbach's thesis). Second, we do this to find solace from our miseries on earth. Third, the cause of our misery is alienation in our everyday lives. Fourth, only communist society can overcome this alienation and thus transcend religion. Now, one possible objection to all of this is that Marx is wrong and traditional theology right: there is a God, who created us, and ordered us to worship him. It is a constant source of wonderment to me that intelligent, educated people can bring themselves to believe any of this, but we'll let that pass. We should just note that if traditional theology is right, Marx took a wrong turn at the start.

Suppose, then, that Feuerbach's thesis is true: human beings invented God. Marx's innovation is to attempt to explain why it is true. Yet should we accept that religion has its source in our misery, and, specifically, the misery of alienation? One difficulty is that even in relatively affluent societies religion continues to exist, even among the more affluent classes. So at least at first sight it is hard to see religion in all its manifestations as a solace. Of course, there are several Marxist-style replies that could be made. First, although some contemporary societies are relatively affluent in material goods, they are still class divided and thus still alienated. So we do all need consolation after all. Second, and distinctly, the existence of religion in class-divided societies is very useful in keeping the workers in check. Distracted by thoughts of heaven, they are less likely to protest about hell on earth. This connects with the theory of ideology. Their social betters have every reason to perpetrate this myth, for their own self-interest. As Engels puts it, describing eighteenth-century England,

> In short, the English bourgeoisie now had to take part in keeping down the 'lower orders', the great producing mass of the nation, and one of the means employed for that purpose was the influence of religion. (*SUS* 22)

While we might note that this portrayal of the workers as the unwitting dupes of a bourgeois conspiracy is hardly edifying, it could be true. Yet even if it is, it doesn't follow that religion's function is a solace, for here it is represented as a means of control. So we should note that Feuerbach's thesis that man invented God is detachable from Marx's hypothesis concerning why we have done this. Thus we may conjecture that something else might explain why we have invented religion. Perhaps it has something to do with our need to explain the world around us. Perhaps it answers some other need that Marx ignored. This is a point we will see made a number of times in the following pages. It is related to the keystone idea of Marx's early writings: that labour, or productive activity, is man's primary form of engagement with the world. This claim will come under further examination shortly.

Turning now to Marx's account of alienation and alienated labour, we must, again, admit that it is very impressive, and contains much of enduring worth. The exact conditions of production he describes may now be relatively rare in Western Europe, but they may be endemic throughout the developing world. Here I want to raise just two points, which will be examined in more detail later, in the discussion of communism. First, although Marx associates alienated labour with capitalist economic organization, it is less clear that capitalism really is the problem. For certain aspects of alienated labour could be a feature of any highly mechanized production process, whether used under communism or capitalism.

In reply it may be said that the division of labour need not be alienating in itself; it is only so when it leads to de-skilling (as was acknowledged earlier). Capitalism encourages this process, at least at certain times in the search for profits, while communism would have no need to. This is a fair point, even though untested. But it still leaves us with a second problem. Marx does very little to tell us what non-alienation would be like. In this instance, while the critique of capitalism may be persuasive, what we are meant to do about it is left very unclear. In essence this is the criticism that Marx simply does not tell us enough about the nature of human emancipation. The same remarks could be repeated concerning Marx's critique of the money and credit system: true, very true, but please tell us what else to do.

Finally, some remarks about Marx's critique of liberalism. Essentially he identifies liberalism with the grant of rights; most interestingly the rights to liberty, equality, security, and property. Here the criticism is that these are rights to guarantee independence and protection from each other. This both presupposes, and reinforces the picture of human beings as isolated atoms, perpetually potential threats to each other. The Marxist point is that this may be an accurate account of how human beings have been conditioned to act under capitalism, but it is no means an essential feature of human existence.

In recent years numerous critics of liberalism have resurrected, or quite possibly reinvented, this argument. Feminist critics, for example, see the liberal system of justice and rights as embodying particularly male confrontational and competitive assumptions about human nature. But, so say some feminists, the human good life is a co-operative one, based on ideas of mutual care, not justice. So not only does the system of rights fail to support flourishing human communities, it actually stands in the way, preventing us enjoying fully human relations.

Let us consider two types of reply. One is to say that human beings are competitive and confrontational, and that history bears this out. Anything else is merely wishful thinking. Is this right? It may be, but it is hard to know how to argue that human life must always be like this. So a second, more moderate, reply may be more convincing. This is simply to observe that we don't know that the egoist picture is false. Given this, we had better insist upon our liberal rights. By analogy, when I double lock my front door at night it is not because I believe that my house will be burgled if I do not— even though, as it happens, I do live in a high crime area. Rather it is that I do not know that I will not be burgled, and cannot rely on the moral good will of all of those who may pass by. Consequently double locking is a kind of insurance. We need to take precautions not because no one can be trusted but because a very small proportion of people cannot be. Defenders of liberal rights make the same point. We need these rights, just in case. It is simply taking too much of a risk to think we can live without them. Too much trust is gross imprudence.

Yet the romantic strain in the opposing line is appealing. A society in which we need to protect ourselves like this is not the best society we can imagine, and surely we can hope for something better. To which the defender of rights will reply:

hope all you like, but don't give up your rights in the meantime.

But we should conclude this section on a more positive note. The force of Marx's early writings is to question the liberal democratic complacency that we find in much of the developed world. As we have seen, Marx's thought has much in common with the growing anti-capitalist movement. This shouldn't be a surprise as he was one of its inspirations, but it helps us to see the continuing relevance and fertility of his thought. Here are some examples.

First, the critique of money, from the 1844 Manuscripts, is perhaps best read as a critique of commodification: the fact that more and more of the things we value are turned into commodities to be bought and sold in the marketplace. Selling children for adoption over the internet is a prominent recent example, but other examples abound. Top-class amateur sport barely exists any more, while stories about football clubs appear on the business pages every day. Education is increasingly driven by issues about financial resources and accounting. An enormous army of people are employed to care for the infant children and elderly parents of others. 'Value' now almost means 'price', or even 'bargain price'. Less and less is given out of love, an instinctive sense of duty, or goodwill, and more and more is sold or exchanged for economic advantage.

Second, Marx took great pains to draw attention to the power of large corporations, especially large financial corporations, who in their commercial decisions may even have the power of life and death over the individuals they decide not to employ, or to whom they refuse to extend credit. Although in the developed world this is somewhat counterbalanced by protection from the state, there are many places where this is not so.

Third, although we may not have been convinced by Marx's argument that in a good society we would not need rights against each other, nevertheless we should agree with him that rights guarantee nothing. I earlier used the example of illegal pay differentials to make the point, but I could have equally used examples of racial discrimination, or discrimination on grounds of religion or class. In theory all of these violate rights, but it all still goes on. We need deeper change.

And we can extend this to a fourth point. Exactly the same issues arise in relation to democracy. While, of course, being included in the electorate is a great advance over being excluded, what it will do for you in practice is another thing altogether. It may have no influence whatsoever in the spheres that matter in everyday life: the workplace; the family. Taking control over one's own life needs more than the liberal rights, even including the right to vote. Once we have achieved the liberal rights we cannot rest. The fight to make them effective may be a long and difficult one. Reminding us of this is part of Marx's legacy, even if he would not have wanted to put the point exactly like this himself.

Theory of history

The theory of history, as presented here, starts from the claim that human productive power tends to develop throughout history, and that forms of society rise and fall as they further or frustrate that growth. More specifically, and of chief interest in his analysis, Marx claims that there will come a time when capitalism will fetter the further development of the productive forces, and as a result it will come to an end, to be replaced by communism.

This is a powerful brew of ideas. But questions can be raised about every link in the argument. Once we start, it is all in danger of unravelling into thin air. Let us begin at the end. Suppose, for the sake of argument, we accept everything, except the last point. Once capitalism falters, why is it that it should be replaced with communism? What argument or evidence does Marx have for this claim? Certainly he states it often enough, but repetition, alas, is not argument even if it is often mistaken for it. However, there are some explicit arguments. Communism, we are told, is growing in the womb of capitalism, just as capitalism was growing in the womb of feudalism. But how convincing is this? After all, Marx also tells us that anarchy of production is also developing under capitalism, and so is the poverty of the workers. Consequently lots of things are growing in the womb of capitalism. So why pick out potentially communist forms of economic analysis for special attention?

Rosa Luxemburg famously attributed to Engels a greater degree of caution: that our alternatives were 'socialism or barbarism'. But still we can ask: why only these two choices—unless barbarism is simply a catch-all term to cover everything except socialism. In truth, Marx predicted the arrival of communism very early in his career; as early as 1843, some years before he developed the main lines of his theory of history. In other words his prediction was not initially derived from the theory, but rather the theory was designed to support a prediction Marx had already made. But he never properly seems to have faced the question of whether the theory of history really does provide a grounding for this prediction.

And things get worse. Does the theory even support the prediction that capitalism will ever come to an end, independently of the question of what may replace it? Marx's explicit statement on this is that every economic structure will eventually fetter the development of the productive forces. Yet he seemed to have excluded communism from this. Why shouldn't it be capitalism that lasts for ever, gently adapting itself to the developing productive forces? Marx's arguments that this cannot be so are based on the falling rate of profit, and ever-worsening crises. But so far capitalism has proved able to weather its storms, and, as we shall see, the law of the falling rate of profit is hard to sustain. From the fact that capitalism is a historical phenomenon (it had a beginning), and is a contingent phenomenon (it doesn't exist by nature or necessity) nothing follows about capitalism having to come to an end. Marx does not give adequate grounds to believe that capitalism must eventually fetter the productive forces.

So Marx makes two predictions that do not seem to follow from the basic theory of historical materialism. This yields a startling result: one can believe Marx's theory of history, yet argue that within this theory there is no good reason to think that capitalism will end, or, if it does, that it will be replaced by communism. This would make one a very peculiar sort of follower of Marx, but is an entirely coherent position.

But what about the theory itself? Nothing I have said so far is intended to cast doubt on the main claims that history is the story of the development of human productive power, or that societies rise and fall on the basis of whether they further or impede that growth. So we should look at this now.

Much of the weight of the theory comes down to the following claim: that should a form of society frustrate the growth of the productive forces, then, eventually, that society will give way. Now this may be true, and certainly supporters of Marx have tried hard to establish it. But let us consider a (fictional) example. Imagine a society of great class division. A small aristocracy has both wealth and power, and is protected in its privilege by a strong, well-paid, military. The remainder of the people, who do most of the work, are relatively impoverished. However their sense of community is so strong that they do not resent their place in society, and their religious belief further supports their acquiescence. They see their rulers as social betters, entitled to their advantages.

Suppose, too, that the development of the productive forces has stagnated. The members of the ruling class have no incentive to innovate, benefiting as they do from existing arrangements, and seeing no need to change. Any attempt to develop new technology is quickly snuffed out. For let us suppose that all rightly see technical change as a huge threat to their existing way of life.

Here, then, the productive forces are fettered. Marxist theory predicts that eventually the productive forces must break free. But now we must ask: why? If everyone is reasonably content, why must there be change? In response it might be said that sooner or later discontent would seep in. A food shortage one year might lead to famine; a second year may lead the workers to question their leaders and to resent their exploitation, and begin to look for ways of improving their situation. At this stage attempts to develop the productive forces may be tried out again, and this time perhaps, they will succeed. The existing social order may then start to crumble.

This may sound plausible enough. But is there any reason to believe that, sooner or later, things *must* work out like this? The argument is that, at bottom, the human needs to eat, to find shelter, and so on are so important that they dissolve all other considerations. Needs to produce must be met.

Perhaps in the long run nothing else can compete with our need simply to survive, and it is this need that drives the relentless progress of the forces of production, revolutionizing society as it goes. But do we not have other needs too? Once more we have found that Marx places enormous reliance on an idea involving labour and production: that the most essential human activity is to labour in order to meet our material needs. I shall postpone further consideration of these claims for a few pages, while we remind ourselves of the value of Marx's contribution to the theory of history.

Marx without doubt had a grand vision. The driving force of history is our search to satisfy our material needs. As the attempt to satisfy our existing needs engenders new needs, this is a process potentially without end. On this view economics is at the root of history. Now, although I have raised some difficulties for this theory, and for the implications Marx tries to draw from it, I have not shown it is false. So for all we know Marx might be right. But even if he is strictly speaking wrong, it is hard to deny that he has transformed our understanding of history. What does drive history? Big ideas? Great individuals? Probably these do have some role to play. But the massive influence of economic forces can hardly be denied, whatever else needs to be included. The real question is whether Marx had the whole truth, or only a major portion of it.

And we must also not forget that it is Marx, above all, who brought us to see the present in historical perspective. Capitalism has not existed for all time; it developed out of other economic conditions. Perhaps it will not last for ever either. We must, at least, remain alive to this possibility, and thank Marx for drawing it so firmly to our attention.

Economics

Marx's economics, we saw, are based on the labour theory of value, and this, in turn, led to his most striking contribution, the theory of surplus value, which shows that capitalist profits depend on the exploitation of the worker. Furthermore, the labour theory of value allows us to understand that capitalism inevitably involves a trade cycle, and, perhaps most crucially of all, a falling rate of profit which, together with ever-deepening crises, brings about its demise. Everything seems to hold together beautifully. But, unfortunately, things are not always as they seem. For at the centre is a massive void. Although he attempts some lengthy arguments, in the end Marx gives us no good reason to believe that the labour theory of value is true, and these days very few economists will defend it. Now, you might say, economists are members, or at least representatives, of the ruling class, and thus bound to dismiss it. Marx's theory of ideology predicts as much! But the point is that some of the strongest criticisms have been made or endorsed by Marxist economists, who were looking for reasons to believe the theory, and failed to find them.

What then are the problems? For present purposes we can divide them into two types. First, there are what we could call the fussy problem cases. In real economies there are many goods which have prices that the labour theory of value seems to have difficulty explaining. Some of Picasso's sketches took seconds, but are worth tens of thousands of pounds. Fine wines become more valuable as they get older; mediocre wines lose value, typically, even if stored in exactly the same conditions. Uncultivated land can be immensely valuable, even though it contains absolutely no labour at all. If a single act of labour produces both a plank of wood, and wood shavings, sold for use as pet animal bedding, how can we apportion the labour between the plank and the shavings in a way that explains why the plank is so much more valuable?

Now, supporters of the labour theory of value rarely take these problem cases very seriously. The theory can be turned, twisted, modified, and redefined to make these problems go away, if one tries hard enough. But there is a more fundamental problem. The key foundational claim for Marx is that labour is the source of all value and all profits. But what was the argument for that? It seems obvious, especially in simple cases, but seeming obvious is not enough. We need a reason. The fact is that although Marx makes some attempts he doesn't provide anything that stands up. So aside from the plausible illustrations he provides, there is no basis for the claim that labour has this special role.

Of course, the fact that the claim is not defended successfully does not show it is false. So economists attempted to formulate the theory in a form where it could be tested. But what happened is very interesting. Once the theory is formulated in mathematical terms it turns out that there is nothing special about labour. That is to say, if one wanted, one could present a 'corn theory of value', an 'oil theory of value'; a 'steel theory of value', or indeed any theory of value at all. A steel theory of value would claim that steel is the source of all value. It also has the remarkable quality that it creates more value than it costs, and thus all capitalist profit comes from the 'exploitation' of steel. Economists would now argue that this is no less justified than the labour theory of value.

The obvious reply is that this claim is absurd. All goods contain labour. They don't all contain steel. So how can steel be the source of all value? But, unfortunately, this argument equally condemns the labour theory of value. For as we have seen, not all goods do contain labour. Uncultivated land was the example. Another might be goods on a fully mechanized production line, which contain no immediate labour. Of course there are traces of 'dead' labour further back—the machines on the production line may contain labour. However, this is not so with uncultivated land, and in any case a similar point can be made about steel, or even the corn in the worker's belly. In sum, surprising as it sounds, from the point of view of economics there is a nothing special about labour.

How, then, do we answer Marx's question? How, in general, is profit possible? I'm not sure. Perhaps by taking advantage of opportunities that are not available to, or seen by, everyone. It is often said that in perfect competition there are no profits (something we may be seeing with respect to commerce on the internet which comes closer to the conditions of perfect competition than any other market we have seen). The point, though, is that even if we cannot easily explain the existence of profit, we should not settle for Marx's theory if there are deep flaws within in.

So the labour theory of value does not explain the source of profit. Consequently the law of the declining rate of profit fails too, for that starts from the assumption that only labour can create value. Does it also follow that workers are not even exploited? Here opinions differ. Some have argued that once the labour theory of value falls there is no basis left for the charge that workers are exploited. But others believe that there is still a strong argument to be made. Suppose you work eight hours a day. Imagine that there is nothing you can buy with your wage that took more than a total of four hours to make. There appears, then, a clear sense in which you have lost something in this. We can say, surely, that there has been an unequal exchange of labour. Someone else is getting the benefit of some of your labour. The truth of this does not depend on any particular theory of value or profit.

Now, is it true that workers under capitalism are exploited in this sense? For the affluent workers of developed economies, probably not. Most Western workers can command more hours of labour than they have to work; provided it is the labour of Third World workers. A day's Western wages might buy you weeks of an Indian or Chinese labourer's work. These are the truly exploited (although who is the exploiter is a more subtle question); and often work in exactly the condition Marx wrote about in the England of the mid-nineteenth century.

Here, then, is one advantage of a broadly Marxist approach to economics. It gives us insight into how people in developed economies exploit the people elsewhere with whom they trade. What else? Joan Robinson, the British economist and follower of Keynes, wrote a short book on Marxist economics first published in the 1940s. As a Keynesian she was, at that time, in the minority among economists and an opponent of the current orthodoxy. So her praise of Marx does have something of 'my enemy's enemy' about it. Nevertheless her analysis remains acute. While she sees nothing of merit in the labour theory of value, she argues that Marx's analysis of capitalism is nevertheless devastating. The insights she identifies include the observation that capitalism depends for its existence on a class of workers who have nothing to sell but their labour power. Capitalism, thus, is not 'the order of nature', and neither is it based on a harmony of interests between worker and capitalist. Rather there is a constant struggle over the nature and conditions of work, and how the surplus is to be divided. And although Robinson would not agree that labour is the source of all value, she does think that this is a way of saying something very important. Capitalists often defend their profits on the basis that it is only because they contribute capital that production can even take place. But Robinson replies: it is the capital that is required; not the capitalist. Owning capital is not a way of being productive. This, ultimately, is the Marxist anti-capitalist insight. Finally, she was especially impressed with Marx's account of the labour market and the industrial reserve army, and his view that, in contrast to classical economics, the idea of equilibrium in the market is a mirage. The trade cycle is with us to stay. Marx's long-term dynamic analysis, she plausibly argues, runs rings round the feeble apologists for capitalism.

Communism

We have seen earlier that Marx was not justified, even in terms of his own theory, in his prediction that communism would follow capitalism. Yet communism, as described, could still be an overwhelmingly attractive image of how society might be organized. So should we sign up to the ideal (worrying about how we might get from here to there later)? Alternatively, we might question whether it really is a coherent ideal after all. Here are four difficulties.

The first is the best known. Marxist communism even if achieved would inevitably break down, it is often said, because we are naturally selfish. We simply cannot behave as Marx would have us do. This objection comes in various strengths. At one extreme the thought is that we are only self-interested, at bottom, and only really care about ourselves. On this view the miracle of capitalism is that it can harness this self-concern for the general good, for the best way to serve one's own interests is to provide goods which serve other people's interests. 'Private vices' generate 'public virtues'. Communism, in contrast, gets all the incentives wrong.

The official Marxist response to this is that we simply do not know it to be true. While it may well be a fair account of how people behave under capitalism, we should note that capitalism encourages and reinforces this type of behaviour. Under communism everything will be different.

Now it must be acknowledged that there is something at least in the first half of this, and that we don't know how we would behave under Marxist communism. Yet the system does have great risks. We do not need to assume anything as strong as the claim that we are all dedicated, grasping, egoists to see this. Rather a tendency to favour our own interests when they come into conflict with others may be enough to sow the seed of disaster. As Trotsky noted, in commenting from exile on Stalin's planned economy, even a benevolent, wise or well-intentioned planner 'will rarely forget himself'. The point is not to say that planners are necessary corrupt or incompetent; but simply that they cannot fail to see things from the point of view of how they, personally, may be affected by their own decisions. Any economy with large elements of planning will be vulnerable.

The second difficulty for any non-capitalist economy is co-ordination. Such problems would afflict both the planned economy, and the 'free-form' economy of hunting and criticizing. The problems with the latter are obvious. If we all work just as we 'have a mind', how can we assure that essential tasks will be completed? The answer is that we cannot. This is not a feasible suggestion, and probably was never intended to be so.

But it may be more surprising to hear that the planned economy would also fail to co-ordinate things properly. After all, is this not its entire *raison d'être*, in contrast to the anarchy of capitalism? Yet just because it has this goal, it certainly doesn't follow that it can achieve it, and the work especially of Frederick von Hayek has brought this out.

The now well-known point is that the market is a fantastic information exchange. Changing prices are signals of shortage and surplus. Furthermore, the capitalist market gives people an incentive to respond to these signals in the search to maximize profits (private vices, public virtues again). Take away the market and the profit motive and you remove both signal and incentive. However skilled the planner, it is impossible to gain the quantity of fine-grained information about consumer demand and changing market conditions that even a small market automatically produces. But even if we did have this information, responding efficiently also relies on a level of good will and power we are unlikely to see. Despite its apparent attractions a planned economy just cannot do what it is designed for.

The third problem is one that would barely have occurred to anyone in the nineteenth century, but has been increasingly prominent since. The resources of the natural world are not inexhaustible. We take this thought for granted, but it seems not to have struck Marx. As a result there may be limits to the level of production we can achieve, even given increasing human ingenuity. There may just not be enough raw material in the world to achieve sustainable abundance for all. Now, much depends on what, in the end, abundance means. But the natural environment produces a hard constraint on what can be achieved, and if sufficient abundance cannot be produced, one of the key conditions of communism fails.

Finally, we must discuss what may well be the deepest problem of all. Much of Marx's argument is premised on the theory that previous societies are divided on a class basis, and the explanation of class division is economic. From this it seems to follow that if we can produce conditions in which there need not be a squabble over economic matters, then there is no reason for classes to form or exist, and thus we have the background to the creation of a classless society. So here is the claim. The basis on which we form ourselves into collective actors is economic. But is this right? Clearly in the real world we do see groups opposing each other on various grounds. Race, religion, nationality, and gender have all created division and struggle. The Marxist reply to this is that all these other struggles, at root, have an economic basis. Yet, in the end, this seems merely dogmatic. Why should it be that other things are not as important to us, as human beings? Just as wealthy families may find plenty to quarrel about, a society of economic abundance may be divided too. Groups may form on any number of lines, and so divisions may assert themselves even in economic paradise. These divisions could be just as deep and potentially destructive as economic classes. Indeed what we have seen in Eastern Europe is that non-economic divisions—ethnic, religious—were suppressed only by highly authoritarian regimes, which controlled their people through fear and an iron hand. Once that authority subsided, ethnic division and hatred surfaced with a ferocity that few in the West had anticipated. The lesson seems to be that human beings are more complicated than the Marxist picture assumes.

Human nature

I have argued that Marx has not given us sufficient reason to believe his two grand theories: the theory of surplus value; and historical materialism. Furthermore, he has not given a workable account of post-capitalist society. All these difficulties share a common root: Marx's account of human nature. Of the many things that Marx says or implies about human nature and its potential, two are most important for present concerns. One concerns human 'universality', the other productive activity.

First, Marx seems to assume that it is possible to be a universal human being in a particular sense, at least in post-capitalist society. When economic divisions have fallen away, we will be left with fellow-feeling for all human beings. Based on a form of solidarity for all human beings which transcends barriers of race, religion, nationality, and so on, we can develop a co-operative, all-inclusive, society. This is anticipated in some remarks in the *Communist Manifesto*:

> The Communists are . . . reproached with desiring to abolish countries and nationalities. The working men have no country. We cannot take from them what they have not got. . . . National differences and antagonisms between peoples are daily more and more vanishing. . . . The supremacy of the proletariat will cause them to vanish still faster. (M. 260)

Note, too, how the *Manifesto* ends: 'WORKING MEN OF ALL COUNTRIES, UNITE!' (M. 271).

But as we asked at the end of the last section, is it really possible for such antagonisms to dissolve away? Could it be essential to some people's self-conception that they live in opposition to some other group? Could there be an ineliminable 'tribal' element that makes universal co-operation impossible? The evidence from the world around us is that our sentiments are much more limited than Marx needs if international communism is to be a realistic aspiration. For my own part I would like to remain optimistic and hope Marx is right about human nature (if not the desirability of international communism). But we are hardly at a point in human history where we can claim this to be so, with any confidence.

Now to the second issue. Right from the start we saw Marx present the idea that the essential human activity is productive activity, specifically labour. This, then, appears first in the Early Writings, yet also provides the grounding for both Marx's economic theory and his theory of history. Labour is the source of all economic value, and is also the driving force of history. But does labour have the importance Marx supposes?

If one had to stand there and pick out a single 'essential human activity', then 'productive activity', broadly construed, looks like a very plausible candidate indeed. But why suppose that there is one essential human activity? Marx says, early in the *German Ideology*:

> Men can be distinguished from animals by consciousness, by religion, or anything else you like. They begin to distinguish themselves from animals as soon as they begin to produce their means of subsistence. (M. 177)

True, this is very clever, but it doesn't really settle anything. Why can't we say that all the things mentioned, and others such as language, are essential to us?

So let us suppose that we accept this multiplicity. What follows? Although it may be too strong to say that anything strictly follows, it may support a certain scepticism about Marx's image of communism. For Marx assumes that once we have achieved material abundance we are in a position to transcend our most important division—class division—and achieve communism without 'the old filthy business' starting again. (*German Ideology*, M. 187) But if production is only one of a number of vital human activities this may not be the case. For if we are divided on religious, philosophical, national or even linguistic grounds, we may find that we are still divided in communism. And we will be divided on an issue that goes deep; as far back as the essence of human nature.

Furthermore, if other things than our productive nature are essential to us, then it will be much harder to maintain Marx's theory of history, which, essentially, relies on our productive needs dominating all other needs. Perhaps, for religious reasons, for example, we might impede the development of the productive forces, for fear that development will threaten our traditional way of life. So for several reasons we now see why the assumption that human beings are essentially productive (and that this is their only essential feature) is so vital for Marx. And we can also see why its rejection is so damaging.

Conclusion

So, as I said, Marx's grandest theories are not substantiated. But he is not to be abandoned. His writings are among the most powerful in the Western intellectual tradition, and, true or false, they are to be appreciated and admired. But further, he does say many true and inspiring things. His work is full of insight and illumination. We have found many such examples. Marx remains the most profound and acute critic of capitalism, even as it exists today. I said at the outset: we may have no confidence in his solutions to the problems he identifies, but this does not make the problems go away.

Guide to references and further reading

As mentioned in the Introduction, the best starting place for reading Marx is the collection edited by David McLcllan, cntitlcd *Karl Marx: Selected Writings*, 2nd edn. (Oxford: Oxford University Press, 2000). Wherever possible, references to this edition of Marx's works are given in the text in the form (M. 368). In some cases I have quoted texts from Marx which are not included in McLennan. For *Capital* Volume 1 I have used the Penguin paperback edition, first published in 1976. This is referred to in the text in the form (*Capital* 454). Certain of Marx's Early Writings, not included in McLellan, are quoted from Lucio Colletti (ed.) *Karl Marx: Early Writings*, (Harmondsworth: Penguin, 1975). These appear as (Colletti 285).

From McLennan I would especially recommend the selections from the *Economic and Philosophical Manuscripts, The German Ideology, The Communist Manifesto, Preface to a Critique of Political Economy, Capital*, and *The Critique of the Gotha Programme*. Equally highly recommended is Engels' *Socialism: Utopian and Scientific*. It is available either as a separate pamphlet; in various editions of Marx/Engels Selected Works; or on the internet archive www.marxists.org. Where I have quoted this text, I have used the Russian Progress Press edition, first published in 1954, and referred to here in the following form (*SUS* 15).

For a lively account of Marx's life, which gives a great sense of how he lived, see the biography by Francis Wheen, *Karl Marx* (London: Fourth Estate, 1999). For a more scholarly account, see David McLellan, *Karl Marx: His Life and Thought* (London: Macmillan, 1973).

I have been influenced a great deal in my reading of Marx's Early Writings, and their philosophical background by Sidney Hook's *From Hegel to Marx* (New York: Humanities Press, 1950). For other helpful accounts of the texts, see David McLennan, *Marx Before Marxism* (London: Macmillan, 1970) and John Maguire, *Marx's Paris Writings*

(Dublin: Gill and Macmillan, 1972). Allen Wood, *Karl Marx* (London: Routledge, 1981), contains a good discussion of the Early Writings, as well as discussions of other topics.

The selections and commentary on Robert Owen are taken from A. L. Morton, *The Life and Ideas of Robert Owen* (London: Lawrence and Wishart, 1962 and 1968). The sections quoted here are reprinted in Michael Rosen and Jonathan Wolff (eds.) *Political Thought*, 23–6 (Oxford: Oxford University Press, 1999). This reader also contains a number of relevant short selections from Marx and Engels. For an account of the utopian socialists see Leszek Kolakowski, *Main Currents of Marxism* Volume 1 (Oxford: Oxford University Press, 1978), chapter 10. This book contains much interesting further reading on topics discussed here. The quotation from Eduard Bernstein's, *Evolutionary Socialism* (1899) is from the 1961 edition published by Shocken Books, New York.

A very clear and helpful introduction to Marxist economics is Paul Sweezy, *The Theory of Capitalist Development* (New York: Monthly Review Press 1942, 1970). The work of Joan Robinson discussed in the text above is *An Essay on Marxian Economics* (London: Macmillan, 1942). The interpretation of Marx's theory of history presented here relies very heavily on G. A. Cohen *Karl Marx's Theory of History*, 2nd edn. (Oxford: Oxford University Press, 2001).

Terrell Carver has written a number of books on both Marx and Engels which are highly relevant to the themes of this book. See, in particular, *Marx's Social Theory* (Oxford: Oxford University Press, 1982), and *The Post-Modern Marx* (Manchester: Manchester University Press, 1998). I particularly recommend chapter 5 of this, which includes a fascinating account of the authorship of the notorious 'hunt in the morning' passage from *The German Ideology*. For a very influential study of 'de-skilling', influenced by Marx's theory of alienated labour, see Harry Braverman, *Labor and Monopoly Capitalism* (New York: Monthly Review Press, 1974).

A sophisticated presentation of the objections to the labour theory of value appears in John Roemer, *A General Theory of Exploitation and Class*

(Cambridge Mass.: Harvard University Press, 1982), esp. 186–8. For a summary of many criticisms of Marx's economics, see Jon Elster, *Making Sense of Marx* (Cambridge: Cambridge University Press, 1985) 127 ff. Elster also contains useful critical discussions of many of the topics covered in this book.

For an account of attempts to put Marxist economic ideas into practice, see Alec Nove *The Economics of Feasible Socialism* (London: George Allen and Unwin, 1983) and *The Economics of Feasible Socialism Revisited* (London: Harper Collins, 1991).

Karl Popper's snipe against Marxism is quoted from his book *Conjectures and Refutations*, 4th edn. (London: Routledge and Kegan Paul, 1972). His more detailed attack appears in his book *The Open Society and Its Enemies Volume 2: Hegel and Marx*, 5th edn. (London: Routledge, 1966). For a critical look at Marxist theories of class, see Frank Parkin, *Marxism and Class Theory: A Bourgeois Critique* (London: Tavistock Publications, 1979).

Index